Karnie

Building Grammar
Teaching the Basics One Skill at a Time

by
Rhonda Chapman

Cover Graphics
Matthew Van Zomeren

Inside Illustrations
Jack Snider

Publisher
Instructional Fair • TS Denison
Grand Rapids, Michigan 49544

About the Author

Rhonda Chapman is a graduate of Grand Valley State University where she received degrees in special education, elementary education, and reading. She has 13 years experience in the classroom, as well as in home schooling and private tutoring. Rhonda has written many books for Instructional Fair • TS Denison, including *Skills for Young Writers* for grade 6 and *Reading Comprehension* for grade 5.

Credits

Author: Rhonda Chapman
Cover Graphics: Matthew Van Zomeren
Inside Illustration: Jack Snider
Project Director/Editor: Sara Bierling
Editors: Meredith Van Zomeren, Kathryn Wheeler
Production/Layout: Amy Shepard

Standard Book Number: 1-56822-910-0
Building Grammar—Grades 5–6
Copyright © 2000 by Instructional Fair Group, Inc.
a Tribune Education Company
3195 Wilson Dr. NW
Grand Rapids, Michigan 49544
All Rights Reserved • Printed in the USA

Table of Contents

Name _____

A Basketball Hero

There are eight main **parts of speech**:

noun	adjective	adverb
verb	preposition	interjection
pronoun	conjunction	

Name the part of speech for every word that is underlined. Record your answers on the lines below.

[1]Tall and strong,
the [2]boy stands out.
[3]Grinning shyly and looking [4]ahead,
he [5]confidently walks
past the [6]wildly cheering [7]crowd.

Day and night he thinks only [8]of the game—basketball.
[9]It seems to completely consume [10]his life.
[11]In his dreams,
he is a three-point scoring [12]champion.
And while awake,
he [13]diligently strives [14]to perfect his jump shot.
He knows one day he will surely [15]leave his mark.

[16]Now the [17]crowd cheers for him.
Here is his chance [18]to shine, [19]and
suddenly he is living his dream before everyone.
[20]Wow, he sinks the winning [21]basket [22]perfectly
and beautifully.
Tall [23]and strong,
the boy [24]stands out.

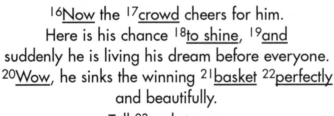

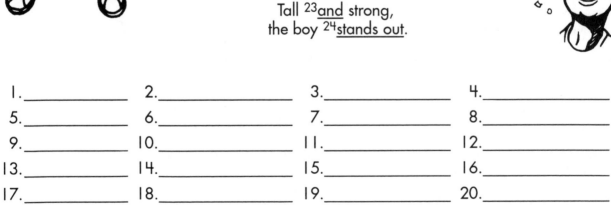

1._____	2._____	3._____	4._____
5._____	6._____	7._____	8._____
9._____	10._____	11._____	12._____
13._____	14._____	15._____	16._____
17._____	18._____	19._____	20._____
21._____	22._____	23._____	24._____

4

Name _____

Who, What, Where?

Nouns are words that name people, places, things, or ideas.
people: *man, Tom, doctor*
places: *store, pharmacy, school*
things and ideas: *flashlight, trust, smile, pain*

Write each noun under the correct category.

president
backyard
kindness
Asia
campsite
park
grace
peace
sister
Keisha
truth
Rafael
White House
office
lady
socialism
music
singer
lawyer
Sweden
pasta
queen
gift
friend
Indiana
desk
astronaut
gym
hoop
zoo

PEOPLE	PLACES	THINGS/IDEAS
1._____	1._____	1._____
2._____	2._____	2._____
3._____	3._____	3._____
4._____	4._____	4._____
5._____	5._____	5._____
6._____	6._____	6._____
7._____	7._____	7._____
8._____	8._____	8._____
9._____	9._____	9._____
10._____	10._____	10._____

Name _____

A Happy Arrival

> **Gender** refers to the sex indicated by a noun. In English, there are four genders: *masculine* (male), *feminine* (female), *neuter* (no sex), and *indefinite* (either sex).
>
> **masculine:** *boy, man, brother*
> **feminine:** *girl, woman, sister*
> **neuter:** *pencil, comb, water*
> **indefinite:** *person, painter, winner*

Rewrite each noun from the Noun Box under the correct category of gender.

IT'S A BOY!

1. _____
2. _____
3. _____
4. _____
5. _____
6. _____

IT'S A GIRL!

1. _____
2. _____
3. _____
4. _____
5. _____
6. _____

Noun Box

father	maiden	bull	cousin	nurse	cola
book	candle	ewe	singer	lad	mask
friend	champion	violin	princess	niece	actress
knight	emperor	seaweed	doctor	uncle	mother

IT'S AN IT!

1. _____
2. _____
3. _____
4. _____
5. _____
6. _____

WHAT IS IT?

1. _____
2. _____
3. _____
4. _____
5. _____
6. _____

Name _____

People, Places, and Things

> **Proper nouns** are the names of specific people, places, or things. They are spelled with a capital letter. Your name is a proper noun. All other nouns are called **common nouns**. Common nouns do not name specific people, places, or things, and are not usually spelled with an initial capital letter.
>
> **proper nouns:** *New Hampshire, Michael Jordan, Central Park*
> **common nouns:** *state, athlete, park*

Write a proper noun for every common noun provided. Then, complete the remaining two noun pairs by providing your own common and proper nouns.

PEOPLE

1. boy — _____

2. girl — _____

3. athlete — _____

4. librarian — _____

5. actor — _____

6. author — _____

7. _____ — _____

8. _____ — _____

PLACES

1. college — _____

2. theater — _____

3. store — _____

4. street — _____

5. city — _____

6. theme park — _____

7. _____ — _____

8. _____ — _____

THINGS

1. game — _____

2. snack — _____

3. song — _____

4. automobile — _____

5. pet — _____

6. book — _____

7. _____ — _____

8. _____ — _____

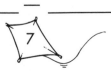

IF87132 *Grammar*

Name _____

More Than One

Plural nouns are nouns indicating two or more people, places, things, or ideas.

1. To form the plural of most nouns, just add **s**.
2. Add **es** to a noun that ends in **s, x, ch, z, sh**, or **ss**.
3. If the noun ends in a **y** that is preceded by a consonant, change the **y** to an **i** and add **es**.
4. Add **es** to a noun that ends in an **o** preceded by a consonant.
5. Add **s** to a noun that ends in an **o** preceded by a vowel.

Change the singular nouns below into plural nouns.

radio _____   family _____

sandwich _____   beard _____

lady _____   mailbox _____

planet _____   cargo _____

kite _____   city _____

country _____   jelly _____

pansy _____   umbrella _____

sound _____   glass _____

buzz _____   dish _____

stereo _____   candy _____

video _____   dress _____

crash _____   hero _____

lunch _____   echo _____

light _____   berry _____

potato _____   candy _____

Name _____

A Red-Letter Day

> **Possessive nouns** show ownership. They describe who or what possesses something. To form a possessive, add **'s** to the end of the noun. If a noun is plural and already ends in an **s**, simply add an apostrophe.
>
> *singular possessive:* Valentine's Day is a great holiday.
> *plural possessive:* I like to look at my classmates' valentines.

Place apostrophes where they belong in each possessive noun below.

It was Valentines Day, and Miss Jacksons class was having a party. One of the partys events was a contest for wearing the most interesting red item. Miss Jackson was impressed with her students participation. Josés t-shirt was red, and Lings socks were too. Tremels hat, Mayas sweater, and Shainas shoes were all red. Some students shirts and jeans were covered with red hearts made from construction paper. But, one boys Valentine outfit stood out above the rest. Grants body was covered from head to toe in red. On his feet he wore little Susies red dragon slippers. Over his clothes he sported his mothers fuzzy red bathrobe, and on his head he wore his grandmas curly, red wig. Everyone in the class agreed that Grants creativity earned him the big heart-shaped box of chocolates.

Name _____

At the Library

> Commas are used to set apart **nouns of address and introductory words or phrases**. A noun of address is what a person's name is called when she is being spoken to.
>
> *Meredith, bring me that book.*
>
> Words like **yes**, **no**, **as usual**, and **well** are called introductory words (or phrases).
>
> *No, I'm busy right now.*

In each sentence below, add commas where necessary.

1. Mrs. Peterson can I check out this book?

2. You would do better Tim with an easier book.

3. Yes I like books about exciting places.

4. However I also enjoy reading biographies about famous people.

5. Don't forget your library card Maria!

6. Please I need this book right now!

7. Well you sure are in a hurry.

8. Reading Dena can be very exciting.

9. Shakespeare Lucy was a great playwright.

10. As usual your library books are late Charlie.

11. By the way your dog chewed the corner of this book.

12. Well Trevor at least the dog didn't eat it.

13. Monica you cannot check out that book.

14. Janelle what kind of books do you like?

15. I prefer mysteries Kwan.

© Instructional Fair • TS Denison

IF87132 *Grammar*

Name _____

All Together

> A **collective noun** names a group of people or things. It may be used as a singular or plural noun, depending on the implied meaning.
> *The family is discussing where to have the reunion. (singular)*
> *The family are all giving their opinions. (plural)*

Write **S** (singular) or **P** (plural) on the line to show how each collective noun is being used.

____ 1. My group is going to Disney World.
____ 2. The crew are all going to work in different places.
____ 3. The litter of puppies are all running helter-skelter.
____ 4. My family are all talking to each other.
____ 5. The class is going on a trip.

Rewrite each sentence, using the correct verb or pronoun from the parentheses.

1. The faculty (is, are) required to turn in their grades by next week.

    _____

2. A number of them (has, have) gone their separate ways.

    _____

3. The team celebrates (its, their) victory.

    _____

4. A couple of students (owns, own) dogs.

    _____

5. The company (is, are) dispersing to their homes.

    _____

6. The boy scout troop (has, have) a bus of its own.

    _____

7. The herd (was, were) returning to their individual stalls.

    _____

8. The crowd was on (its, their) feet.

    _____

Name _____

Illumination

> A **direct object** is a noun or pronoun that follows a transitive verb. It tells what or whom receives the action of the verb. To find the direct object, ask *what* or *whom* after the action verb.
>
> My mom turns on my light to wake me for school.
> (turns on what?)
> My mom wakes me for school by turning on my light.
> (wakes whom?)

In each of the following sentences, underline all the verbs or verb phrases and draw a box around the direct object.

1. When we go camping, we take a lantern.

2. Mom lights candles when the power goes out.

3. I have a nightlight in my bedroom.

4. The flashlight needs two batteries to work.

5. Bright spotlights illuminated the stage during the play.

6. The sun lights and warms our world.

7. Our Christmas bulbs create a lovely glow.

8. Twinkling stars filled the clear evening sky.

9. Several rows of candles on the cake lit the room.

10. Sometimes a full moon illuminates the night all by itself.

11. We save energy at our house by turning off the lights when we leave a room.

12. Turn off the lights when you're done.

13. The parents calmed their children in the dark.

14. In the cave, the small lamp leads the explorers through the blackness.

15. A bright, full moon amazed the stargazers.

Name _____

Our Holiday

> An **indirect object** is a noun or pronoun that names the person or object *to whom* or *for whom (or what)* something is done. To find the indirect object, ask *to* or *for whom* or *to* or *for what* after the action verb.
>
> *Allison bought Timmy a gift.*
> (bought for **whom?** <u>Timmy</u>)
>
> *I gave the charity some money.*
> (gave some money **to what?** <u>the charity</u>)

In each of the following sentences, circle the action verb and underline the indirect object.

1. In the morning, Dad read us a story.

2. Then, Mom served everyone cinnamon rolls and hot cocoa.

3. I gave the cat its favorite food.

4. Then, we gave each other our gifts.

5. Johnny found Mom a big box to open right away.

6. I made my sister a painted sweatshirt.

7. She gave me a diary.

8. Dad made Mom a rocking chair.

9. She knit him a sweater.

10. My sister and brother and I wrote our parents a song.

11. We sang them it, too.

12. Later, Mom cooked the family a delicious dinner.

13. After dinner, we gave Grandma a call.

14. Grandma had sent us presents.

15. Tomorrow we will write everyone who sent gifts thank-you notes.

Name _____

Looking Good!

> A **direct object** is a noun or pronoun that follows an action verb. It tells *what* or *whom* receives the action of the verb. An **indirect object** is a noun or pronoun that names the person or thing *to whom* or *for whom* something is done.
>
> I.O.   D.O.
> *I gave <u>Louise</u> <u>a make-over</u> yesterday.*

In each of the following sentences, underline the direct object once and the indirect object twice. Circle all verbs. (Note: Some sentences do not have an indirect object.)

Louise needed a new look in the worst way.

She asked me to help.

I gave her my suggestions.

First we brushed her hair.

Her wild hair gave the brush a real workout.

Then we pulled her hair back with a tie-dyed ribbon.

"Wash your face too," I suggested.

Next, I found her an outfit that matched.

I loaned Louise a tie-dyed shirt.

Mom gave me some glittery nail polish for my friend's manicure.

We filed and buffed her nails.

Louise offered me her fingers (and toes) for painting.

When we finished, she wore a huge smile.

Louise showed everyone her improvements.

Shall I give you a make-over too?

14

Name _____

On-the-Road Adventure

> A **noun** is a word that names a person, place, thing, or idea.
> A **verb** is a word that states an action or a state of being. Some words can act as either nouns or verbs.
> **noun:** a bark, a ride, a snack, love
> **verb:** to bark, to ride, to snack, to love

In the story below, mark the underlined words **N** (noun) or **V** (verb) to indicate how each word is used in the sentence.

I had to <u>dress</u> by 10:00 a.m. I passed by my yellow <u>dress</u> and slipped on a <u>pair</u> of jeans. I <u>paired</u> them with a tank top. I had to hurry. At 10:30, Dad and I were leaving to <u>canoe</u> and camp at the lake. We had purchased a special <u>canoe</u> from the sporting goods store.

We were on the road for several hours, and I was just beginning to <u>tire</u>, when one of our <u>tires</u> burst. I could hear the air <u>stream</u> out of the tire as Dad moved the car to the side of the road by a <u>stream</u>.

We were miles from anywhere, so we decided to <u>camp</u> right there. Dad set up a <u>camp</u> just off the road in a small clearing with a few trees. I helped him <u>push</u> the car off the road. He put the car in neutral, and I gave it a big <u>push</u> onto the shoulder.

At the camp, we roasted marshmallows and started <u>singing</u> campfire songs. Dad proclaimed my <u>singing</u> better than his.

Write each noun/verb on the lines below. Add four words that can be either a noun or a verb.

_____   _____   _____

_____   _____   _____

_____   _____   _____

_____   _____   _____

verbs

Name _____

On Your Toes!

A **verb** is a word that expresses an action or a state of being.
action: hug, baked, sings
being: is, was, seems

In each of the following sentences, circle the verb and indicate if it is an action (**A**) or a state of being (**B**) verb.

_____ 1. Classical ballet began hundreds of years ago.

_____ 2. Ballet originated in Italy during the Renaissance.

_____ 3. Dancers create graceful patterns using formal, precise movements.

_____ 4. A ballerina is a female dancer.

_____ 5. Ballet dancers point their toes.

_____ 6. A pirouette is a full turn completed on one foot.

_____ 7. Excellent dancers train for many years.

_____ 8. Choreographers arrange the movements that make up the dance.

_____ 9. A tutu, a short, full skirt, is one kind of dancer's costume.

_____ 10. Ballet dancers wear soft leather shoes.

_____ 11. Ballet often tells a story, such as a fairy tale.

_____ 12. The dancers dress in marvelous costumes.

_____ 13. *Swan Lake* is a well-known ballet.

_____ 14. The ballerinas' movements seem swanlike.

_____ 15. Other famous ballets include *Coppelia* and *The Nutcracker*.

Name _____

Make a Blue-Jean Bag

> A **verb** is a word that expresses an action or a state of being.
> Some verbs are preceded by a helping verb.
>
> > *action:* sink, fought, cries
> > *being:* is, are, seemed
> > *helping + verb:* will run, can be, have written

In each of the following sentences, circle the verb. Draw a line from each sentence to the correct bag.

- First, find a pair of old blue jeans.

- Next, locate a pair of scissors with sharp blades.

- You will need some thread, a needle, and a colored bandanna.

- After gathering your supplies, cut the jeans into very short shorts.

- Stitch the short legs closed with your needle and thread.

- Leave about a half-inch below your stitching.

- After the legs have been sewn shut, pull some threads away from the bottom edge of the shorts.

- Now you have created fringe along the edge of your bag.

- Roll the bandanna into a long tie.

- Then run it through the belt loops.

- After you have done that, tie the bandanna in front by the zipper.

- The bag still needs a shoulder strap.

- Use a long narrow strip, cut from one of the legs, as a strap.

- Sew the ends of the strap to the sides of the shorts bag.

- Now your blue-jean bag is finished.

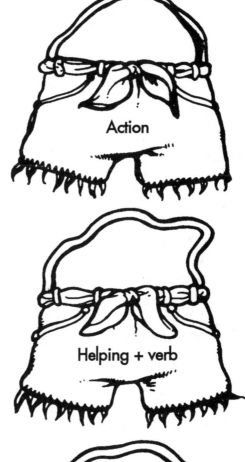

Action

Helping + verb

Being

Name _____

Verb Tents

The **tense** of a verb indicates the time an action takes place.
Present tense indicates action or being that is happening now.
Past tense indicates action or being that was completed in the past. The **future tense** indicates action or being that will take place in the future.

> **present tense:** *Stacey camps outside.*
> **past tense:** *Stacey camped outside.*
> **future tense:** *Stacey will camp outside.*

Fill in the verb tents with the missing verb forms, assuming *he* or *she* is the subject.

present: camp
past:
future:

present:
past: fished
future:

present:
past:
future: will cook

present:
past: roasted
future:

present: place
past:
future:

Over the verbs that are underlined below, indicate each verb's tense with **P** (present), **PA** (past), or **F** (future).

Stacey and her cousin <u>like</u> to do things together. One summer night, they <u>decided</u> to camp in the backyard. They <u>set up</u> a tent and <u>placed</u> their sleeping bags inside. They <u>brought</u> snacks and a portable stereo with them. Of course, they <u>didn't</u> get much sleep. The girls <u>talked</u> all night long. They <u>discussed</u> all the things they wanted to do for the rest of the summer. Finally, they <u>fell asleep</u>. Tomorrow, Stacey and her cousin <u>will pack</u> up their camp and <u>will do</u> something else for fun.

verb tense

Name _____

A Fine Hatch

> The **tense** of a verb indicates the time the action of the sentence takes place. **Present tense** indicates action or being that is happening now. **Past tense** indicates action or being that was completed in the past. **Future tense** indicates action or being that will take place in the future. The auxiliary verb *will* is usually used with the principle verb to form the future tense.
>
> > *present:* Joseph plants corn
> > *past:* Joseph planted corn.
> > *future:* Joseph will plant corn.

Identify the tense of the verb in each sentence: **P** (present), **PA** (past), or **F** (future).

Underline the verb/ verb phrase first.

_____ 1. The mother robin laid her eggs in a nest on our front porch.

_____ 2. Unfortunately, whenever we go through the front door, she leaves her nest.

_____ 3. Yesterday we noticed that there were five blue eggs in the nest.

_____ 4. We have been concerned about the eggs staying warm enough.

_____ 5. The eggs will hatch in about two weeks.

_____ 6. We did not remove the nest from the porch after she hatched her eggs last spring.

_____ 7. I will leave this nest alone since she may return again next spring.

_____ 8. Last spring, four baby birds hatched.

_____ 9. I can't wait to see how many we will have this year.

_____ 10. For now, we are trying to stay away from the porch so the mother bird will stay on her nest and keep those eggs safe.

_____ 11. We will be careful not to touch the birds or the nest.

_____ 12. It is exciting to watch the babies grow.

_____ 13. It won't be long before the new birds will fly away.

IF87132 *Grammar*

Name _____

May I Sit, Set, Lie, or Lay?

> **Lie** means to rest or recline while **lay** means to put or place.
>
> **Sit** means to rest in a seated position while **set** means to place or put something.
>
> **May** is used to ask permission while **can** refers to something you have the physical ability to do.
>
> > *I will **lie** down to rest as soon as I **lay** out some clean clothes for tomorrow.*
> > *Please **sit** down while I **set** the table for dinner.*
> > *Mom says we **may** put up the tent if we **can** figure out how to do it.*

In the following sets of sentences, circle the correct verb.

1. Nancy (lay, laid) a table cloth on the ground and began to unpack the picnic basket.
2. The children's dog (lays, lies) on the grass nearby.
3. Little Kenneth (lays, lies) beside him looking at the fluffy clouds overhead.
4. Troy helped to (lay, lie) the sandwiches on plates.
5. Meanwhile, Rex, the dog, (lays, lies) under the big maple tree.
6. His favorite ball (lays, lies) next to him.

1. It's time to (set, sit) down for lunch.
2. Please (set, sit) the pepper and salt on the table.
3. The baby will (set, sit) in his high chair.
4. The girls want to (set, sit) next to each other.
5. Mom (sets, sits) the food in the middle of the table.
6. She is usually the last one to (set, sit) down.

1. After the picnic, we (can, may) take a walk on the trails.
2. (Can, May) you carry the water bottle?
3. Mom said we (can, may) take the binoculars too.
4. (Can, May) I have the camera?
5. I (can, may) take pretty good pictures.
6. If we hurry, we (can, may) see some interesting wildlife before it gets dark.

Name _____

O Canada!

> The **subject** and **verb** of any clause must agree in number. If a subject is singular, the verb must be singular. If a subject is plural, the verb must be plural.
>
> *The singer (singular) performs (singular) "O Canada."*
> *The singers (plural) perform (plural) "O Canada."*

In the following sentences, decide if the subjects and verbs agree. If they agree, write **YES**. If they do not, write **NO**. Correct the sentences where the subject and verb do not agree.

_____ 1. More than 28 million people lives in Canada.

_____ 2. The government recognizes two official languages.

_____ 3. Some Canadians speaks French.

_____ 4. Others speak English.

_____ 5. Canada are divided into provinces and territories.

_____ 6. The Native Americans makes up approximately two percent of the population.

_____ 7. Many of Canada's schools are run by religious organizations.

_____ 8. Many Canadians enjoy winter activities such as skiing and snowshoeing.

_____ 9. Today, hockey is probably the most popular sport in Canada.

_____ 10. The food of the Canadians is similar to that eaten by Americans.

_____ 11. Many famous actors, authors, and musicians come from Canada.

_____ 12. Canada have six standard time zones.

_____ 13. Just like the United States, there is Rocky Mountains in Canada.

_____ 14. Much of Canada maintains temperatures below 50° F (10° C) year round.

_____ 15. Canada are surrounded by water on three sides.

_____ 16. Toronto, Canada is a popular vacation spot for many tourists.

Name _____

Just Your Average Day

A **regular verb** is one which forms its past and past participle tenses by adding **ed** or **d** to the present tense verb form.

jump, jumped, (have, has, had) jumped
watch, watched, (have, has, had) watched

Write the past and past participle forms of the following verbs.

PRESENT	PAST	PAST PARTICIPLE
1. wait	_____	(have, has, had) _____
2. roam	_____	(have, has, had) _____
3. create	_____	(have, has, had) _____
4. believe	_____	(have, has, had) _____
5. hunt	_____	(have, has, had) _____
6. travel	_____	(have, has, had) _____

Supply your own regular verbs to complete these sentences.

1. The children have _____ to school.

2. They have _____ hard all day.

3. During recess they _____ a game of tag.

4. For lunch they had _____ pizza.

5. In the afternoon, the class _____ the history of Rome.

6. Now the students have _____ home again.

Write one sentence for each verb given.

(skate)_____

(has obeyed)_____

(dance)_____

Name _____

Aberant Actions

An **irregular verb** is any verb that does not form its past and past participle tenses by adding **d** or **ed** to its present tense.

wear, wore, (have, has, had) worn
eat, ate, (have, has, had) eaten

Complete the chart.

PRESENT	PAST	PAST PARTICIPLE (have, has, had)
begin	began	
blow		blown
	did	done
draw	drew	
	drove	driven
fly		flown
forbid	forbade	
	gave	given
go		gone
hide	hid	
	knew	known
lie		lain
ride	rode	
	said	said
shake		shaken
sing	sang	
	spoke	spoken
take		taken
tear	tore	

Name _____

Swimming Lessons

An **irregular verb** is any verb that does not form both its past and past participle tenses by adding **d** or **ed** to its present tense.

shake, shook, (have, has, had) shaken
fight, fought, (have, has, had) fought

Write the past and past participle form of each of the following verbs.

PRESENT	PAST		PAST PARTICIPLE
drink	_____	(have, has, had)	_____
creep	_____	(have, has, had)	_____
freeze	_____	(have, has, had)	_____
hide	_____	(have, has, had)	_____
steal	_____	(have, has, had)	_____
throw	_____	(have, has, had)	_____
weave	_____	(have, has, had)	_____
write	_____	(have, has, had)	_____

Circle the correct verb in each sentence.

1. Many kids have (swimmed, swum) at the high school pool.

2. Mr. Steel has (taught, teached) swimming lessons for years.

3. No one has (wore, worn) bathing caps in any of my classes.

4. We had (dived, doven) into the deep end often.

5. I (feeled, felt) embarrassed when I did a belly flop.

6. We practiced rescuing a person who had (fell, fallen) into the water.

7. Fortunately, no one had (sunk, sunken) to the bottom for real.

8. My relay team had (won, winned) the backstroke race.

9. I (drank, drunk) a lot of pool water.

10. Sara was (thrown, throwed) into the deep end.

Name _____

Pete

> A **contraction** is formed by joining two words. Some contractions are formed by adding the word *not* to a verb. An apostrophe takes the place of the *o* in not, which is dropped.
>
> *do + not = don't*

Write the contraction of the underlined words on the line after each sentence.

1. To meet Pete <u>is not</u> a treat. _____
2. Pete <u>does not</u> eat meat. _____
3. Pete <u>can not</u> eat wheat. _____
4. Pete <u>would not</u> even eat a beet. _____
5. But, <u>do not</u> try to stop Pete from eating sweets. _____

Complete the following equations.

do + not = _____

will + not = _____

should + not = _____

was + not = _____

have + not = _____

are + not = _____

could + not = _____

had + not = _____

has + not = _____

were + not = _____

Add an apostrophe to each contraction below. On the line, write the two words that form each contraction.

1. Pete isnt a sweet kid. _____
2. He cant seem to be nice to others. _____
3. Pete's parents dont know what to do. _____
4. They shouldnt yell. _____
5. They couldnt scold. _____
6. So, they havent done anything. _____
7. Pete doesnt act politely with his teachers. _____
8. He wouldnt consider being kind to his friends. _____
9. Pete hasnt ever been considerate. _____

Name _____

The Night Sky

> A **linking verb** does not show action. It connects a word or words in the predicate to the subject of the sentence. Some very common linking verbs are forms of *to be*: **am**, **are**, **is**, **was**, and **were**. If a verb can be replaced by a form of *to be*, it is usually a linking verb.
>
> *The night sky **is** a very beautiful sight.*

In the following sentences, circle the linking verbs and underline the words that each links.

I am a night-sky watcher.

Where I live, the night sky is extremely dark.

The sky is a blanket of extraterrestrial light.

The stars are jewels on a black-velvet backdrop.

They are the little night lights to guide my way.

Last night, several shooting stars were visible.

As we watched them fall, we were delighted.

Tonight the moon is a ball of light.

Sometimes it is a sliver of brightness.

Not all linking verbs are forms of *to be*. Write **Yes** or **No** next to each sentence below to show if it contains a linking verb.

____ 1. The dark night felt chilly.

____ 2. The girl felt her way through the pitch-black tunnel.

____ 3. The children grew sleepy.

____ 4. We grow lilacs in our yard.

____ 5. Suzie smelled the morning glories.

____ 6. The breeze off the lake smelled wonderful.

Name _____

A Few Famous People

> A **linking verb** does not show action; it connects a word or words in the predicate to the subject of the sentence. Some common linking verbs are forms of *to be*: **am**, **are**, **is**, **was**, and **were**.
>
> A **predicate noun** is a noun following a linking verb. It tells something about the subject and may also be called a subject complement.
>
>   L.V.   P.N.
> *Learning about famous people **is** a fun **hobby**.*

In each of the following sentences, circle the linking verb and underline the predicate noun.

1. Michael Jordan is an amazing basketball player.

2. Steven Spielberg is an award-winning movie director.

3. Harriet Tubman was a brave woman who freed many slaves.

4. The Beatles were popular musicians from England.

5. One of the most loved presidents of the United States is Abraham Lincoln.

6. One impressive female athlete is the ice-skating Michelle Kwan.

7. Charles Lindbergh was the first person to fly non-stop across the Atlantic Ocean by himself.

8. A favorite author of many young people is Gary Paulsen.

9. The *Mona Lisa* is a well-known painting by Leonardo daVinci.

10. One former first lady of the United States of America is Nancy Reagan.

11. Snoopy is the most lovable beagle ever.

12. Theodore Roosevelt refused to shoot a chained bear; this is the origin of the term "teddy bear."

Write four original sentences containing the linking verb noted and a predicate noun.

(is)   1._____

(are) 2._____

(was) 3._____

(were) 4._____

Name _____

Tennis Anyone?

> A **linking verb** does not show action. It connects a word or words in the predicate to the subject of the sentence. Some very common linking verbs are forms of *to be*: **am**, **are**, **is**, **was**, and **were**.
>
> A **predicate adjective** follows a linking verb and describes the subject. It is also known as a subject complement.
>
> L.V.   P.A.
>
> *Successful tennis players **are disciplined**.*

In each of the following sentences, circle the linking verb and underline the predicate adjective.

1. Their game of tennis was challenging.

2. The final game was exciting for the spectators.

3. Both of the players were competitive.

4. The sun was hot above the bleachers.

5. The loudly cheering crowd was huge.

6. Everyone was eager to see the winner claim his prize.

7. Each volley was strong.

8. Finally, one player was thrilled because he won the match.

9. The cash prize was sizable.

10. A win like that is wonderful for any tennis player.

Write five original sentences that contain the linking verb noted and a predicate adjective.

(am)   1. _____

(is)   2. _____

(are) 3. _____

(was) 4. _____

(were) 5. _____

Name _____

The Bear Facts

> A **predicate noun** or **adjective** follows a linking verb and renames the subject.
> *predicate noun: Mike is a bear hunter.*
> *predicate adjective: Mike is brave.*

In each of the following sentences, circle the linking verb and underline either the predicate noun or the predicate adjective, whichever is used. On the line, write **PN** for each predicate noun and **PA** for each predicate adjective.

_____ 1. Bears are mammals.

_____ 2. They are large and powerful animals.

_____ 3. A bear's home is a den.

_____ 4. A den is a cave.

_____ 5. Fully grown bears are strong.

_____ 6. A bear's paw is powerful.

_____ 7. Hungry bears are dangerous.

_____ 8. All bears are short-tempered.

_____ 9. Still, most bears are quite peaceful.

_____ 10. Baby bears are cubs.

_____ 11. When they are born, cubs are surprisingly small.

_____ 12. A mother bear is protective of her cubs.

_____ 13. Bear cubs are playful.

_____ 14. Insects and grubs are delicious cub foods.

_____ 15. Honey is a sweet bear treat.

_____ 16. Bears are excellent fishers.

_____ 17. They are good swimmers too.

_____ 18. A bear's sense of smell is excellent.

Name _____

Amazing Animal Facts

> A **transitive verb** is an action verb that directs action toward a direct object.
> *Mr. McGrady's dog* **chewed** *the shoes.*

In each of the following sentences, underline the transitive verb and circle the direct object.

1. A gila monster stores fat in its tail.

2. The sticky feet of green tree frogs grip smooth, slippery surfaces.

3. A chimpanzee uses sticks to catch bugs.

4. Baby prairie dogs play hide-and-seek.

5. Elephants bury their dead with leaves and dirt.

6. The narwhal may use its tusk for fighting.

7. The addax, a desert antelope, never drinks water.

8. The Etuscan shrew eats three times its own weight each day.

9. Vampire bats drink about a tablespoon of blood a day.

10. An Alsatian dog has forty-four times more smell cells than a human being.

11. The blue whale has eyes as big as footballs.

12. The ground squirrel in the Kalahari Desert uses its tail to shade it from the sun.

13. The tenrec, an insect-eater from Madagascar, uses spit rubbed into the bark of trees to mark its territory.

14. Prairie dogs exchange a "kiss" when they meet in order to find out if they know each other.

15. The sea otter uses a large stone balanced on its stomach to smash open shellfish.

16. A male platypus has poisonous spurs on its back legs.

17. In 1875, a beagle from Switzerland climbed Mont Blanc, the highest mountain in the Alps.

18. A beaver once built a dam that was 2,296 feet (700 m) long.

  30

Name _____

Aunt Sally and Sam

An **intransitive verb** is an action verb that does not have a direct object and does not direct action toward someone or something.
*Parrots **talk** constantly.*
*(**Parrots talk** can stand alone.)*

In the following sentences, underline each intransitive verb and circle each subject.

My Aunt Sally lives up the hill with her five dogs, twelve cats, and talking parrot Sam.

Aunt Sally paints in the early morning and in the late afternoon.

She works in her garden in between.

While she plants, Sam squawks out the window at her.

He screeches until she comes in the house.

In her kind way, she smiles at Sam.

Together they relax with the cats and dogs near the big picture window in the sitting room.

They watch as the sun sets.

Sally hums to her animal friends.

Sam sings along with her.

Another day ends peacefully on Aunt Sally's hill.

Write four original sentences, using the transitive verbs below.

1. (sing) _____

_____

2. (play) _____

_____

3. (work) _____

_____

4. (ride) _____

Name _____

It's Easy Being Green

> A **transitive verb** is followed by a direct object. An **intransitive verb** does not direct action toward an object.
>
> *transitive:* I painted my bedroom green.
> *intransitive:* My sister helped.

Determine if the following sentences are transitive (**T**) or intransitive (**I**). Write your response on the blank before each sentence.

_____ 1. I love to eat big garlic dill pickles on a hot summer day.

_____ 2. Most bullfrogs have bumpy, dark green skin.

_____ 3. Popeye eats spinach to stay tough and strong.

_____ 4. Sour limes make a tasty key-lime pie!

_____ 5. At our house, green jelly beans always get eaten first.

_____ 6. On St. Patrick's Day, many people celebrate the color green.

_____ 7. I like to have green dollar bills in my wallet.

_____ 8. Valuable emeralds are found in beautiful pieces of jewelry.

_____ 9. The cool green grass feels great on my toes.

_____ 10. The pond is decorated with luscious lilypads.

_____ 11. A grasshopper hides in the tall grasses.

_____ 12. Iggie, the pale green iguana, eats flies.

_____ 13. Green lights give permission to go.

_____ 14. A moldy fuzz grows in the refrigerator.

_____ 15. The color green symbolizes envy.

_____ 16. Sam I Am likes green eggs and ham.

_____ 17. Broccoli is good for you.

_____ 18. Making green slime is fun.

Name _____

Happily Ever After

A **participle** is a verb form that can act as an adjective. A **present participle** is the *ing* form of a verb. The **past participle** of most verbs ends in *d* or *ed,* and occasionally *t, en,* or *n.*

> **present:** Fairy tales with enchanted castles and dancing maidens are my favorite.
> **past:** My sister loves the tale of the slain giant.

Underline the participle in each of the following sentences and identify if each one is a present **(PR)** or past **(PA)** participle.

_____ 1. A kiss awakened the sleeping princess, who had been in the tower for a hundred years.

_____ 2. The witch offered Snow White a poisoned apple because she was jealous of the girl's beauty.

_____ 3. The three bears surveyed the broken chair and the bowls of porridge.

_____ 4. Under the moonlight, the dancing couple fell hopelessly in love.

_____ 5. The people mock the self-exalting emperor and his royal new clothes.

_____ 6. Because of her love for her father, Beauty went to live in the enchanted castle.

_____ 7. Rapunzel lets down her flowing hair when the witch calls to her.

_____ 8. In exchange for the maiden's first-born child, Rumpelstiltskin changed the straw into gold on his spinning wheel.

_____ 9. Hansel and Gretel heard the evil witch's voice from within the candied cottage.

_____10. The ugly ogre is fooled by a talking cat in boots and a hat.

_____11. The princess's sleep is disturbed by an annoying pea under her mattresses.

_____12. Thumbelina emerged from the beautiful opening blossom.

Write a short sentence for each participle noted below.

1. (baked) _____

2. (chirping) _____

3. (singing) _____

4. (chosen) _____

verb phrases   Name _____

The Hundred Acre Wood

> A **verb phrase** is a group of words that does the work of a single verb. The phrase includes one principal verb and one or more helping verbs.
>
> *Stories of Winnie-the-Pooh **are set** in the Hundred Acre Wood.*

In each of the following sentences, underline the verb phrase and circle the helping verbs.

1. A.A. Milne was born on January 18, 1882.

2. He is known as the author of the Winnie-the-Pooh stories.

3. His first book, a collection of poems, was entitled *When We Were Very Young*.

4. *We Are Six, Winnie-the-Pooh,* and *The House at Pooh Corner* were written by Milne.

5. These stories were written for his young son.

6. The Pooh stories were illustrated by Ernest Shepard.

7. Milne had used his son's stuffed animals as characters in the stories.

8. One of Milne's characters was based on his son, Christopher Robin.

9. These books have been some of the most popular children's books ever written.

10. Pooh is always eating honey.

11. Eeyore has always been a little glum.

12. In recent years, the stories of Pooh have emerged as children's cartoons and videos.

13. Pooh lovers can purchase Pooh clothes and toys.

14. Pooh has become an internationally recognized figure.

15. A.A. Milne's loveable characters will continue to live in people's hearts forever.

Name _____

Mall Time

> An **infinitive** is a present tense verb and is generally preceded by the word *to*. It may act as a noun, verb, adjective, or adverb.
>
> **To go** *to the mall is great.*
> *I ordered Chinese* **to go** *at the Food Court.*
> *She was happy* **to go** *with us.*
> *I want* **to go** *to the stores.*

Draw a box around the infinitives in each of the following sentences.

1. It's a blast to go shopping at the mall with my best friends.

2. Since we don't drive, our moms are glad to drop us off.

3. We agree on a few stores to check out right away.

4. Leza tries to find the perfect shoes.

5. Beth wants to buy a good book, but Kendra wants to save her money for some earrings.

6. I am determined to purchase a cool hat for my older brother's birthday present.

7. After awhile, our stomachs start to growl, and we have to get something to eat.

8. My friends and I like to eat at the food court.

9. Of course, it's easy to enjoy a yummy lunch with all of the junk food there.

10. We usually try to share our food so that everyone gets to taste a little bit of everything.

11. Before we get ready to leave, we make one last stop at the chocolate shop.

12. Everybody spends a little money to buy the moms some chocolate truffles.

13. We want to show them how much we appreciate their driving us here.

14. I can't wait to come back to the mall again soon.

forms of be

Name _____

Soaring Above the Clouds

> Forms of the verb **be** can be used as linking or helping verbs.
> Linking verbs link the subject to the predicate. Helping verbs are
> added to the front of a verb to "help" it complete an action.
>
> **linking:** *Studying airplanes is Joel's favorite hobby.*
> **helping:** *He is going to the county airshow.*

Write **correct** or **incorrect** on the line to tell whether the form of be is used correctly in each sentence.

1. You be tired after a long plane flight. _____
2. The flight is going to take off late. _____
3. She been waiting for the plane to land. _____
4. The plane has been cleaned and stocked with food. _____
5. We are going to fly to Hawaii. _____
6. Be you frightened of flying? _____
7. They are boarding the plane. _____
8. The pilot is turning on the no-smoking sign. _____

Write **linking** or **helping** on the line to tell how the form of be is used in each sentence.

1. Joel is flying over Lake Michigan. _____
2. The weather is good. _____
3. Aviation is Joel's favorite subject. _____
4. The plane was climbing in the air. _____
5. All the passengers' lap belts were fastened. _____
6. I am hoping to take flying lessons. _____
7. My favorite airplane is the P–51. _____
8. I have been waiting to go to the airshow. _____
9. Airplanes are used by the military and civilians. _____
10. The Blue Angels is the U.S. Navy's famous flying team. _____
11. Playing flying games on the computer is a hobby of mine. _____
12. Inventors have been building flying machines for a long time. _____

Name _____

Sweet Tooth

> Forms of the verbs *do* and *have* can be used as main verbs or helping verbs. Helping verbs are added to the front of another verb and "help" it complete an action.
>
> **main verb:**   *I do my work*
>   *I had a snack.*
>
> **helping verb:** *I do try to eat well.*
>   *I have eaten an entire cake.*
>
> **Note:** Don't use *of* when you mean to say *have*.
>
> *They should of known her better. (incorrect)*
> *They should have known her better. (correct)*

Write **main** or **helping** on the line to tell how the underlined verb in each sentence is used.

1. Mom <u>did</u> tell me to stop eating sweets. _____

2. Maybe I should not <u>have</u> had that second donut. _____

3. Kate <u>had</u> a new recipe. _____

4. I <u>did</u> the dinner dishes. _____

5. Mike <u>does</u> have a weakness for chocolate. _____

6. Betsy <u>has</u> liked caramel in the past. _____

7. I <u>have</u> four different kinds of gum. _____

8. Dad <u>does</u> tell me not to eat so much candy. _____

9. I <u>did</u> the most eating. _____

10. Becky <u>has</u> eaten too much food. _____

On the line, show how to correct the verbs in each sentence. Not all sentences are incorrect.

Example: I having a good time.   <u>I am having a good time.</u>

1. Who done the most work?   _____

2. We having several cupcakes.   _____

3. This chocolate has a peculiar taste.   _____

4. I have did something nice for him.   _____

5. He should of saved me some pie.   _____

6. Charlie is having a cookie-tasting party.   _____

7. Kate and Mike have did me a favor.   _____

8. Those nut clusters would have been a good choice.   _____

Hot Wheels

The **perfect tenses** communicate a sense of continuing action. The present tense shows action begun in the past and completed in the present. It is formed by adding *has* or *have* to the past participle.

> *Dave has passed his road test.*
> *His friends have congratulated him.*

The past perfect tense shows action begun and completed in the past. It is formed by adding *had* to the past participle.

> *He had practiced hard all summer.*

The future perfect tense shows action begun in the past or present that will be completed in the future. It is formed by adding *will have* to the present participle.

> *Dave will have gotten a new car by next winter.*

Show the tense of the perfect verb in each sentence by writing **PR** (present), **P** (past), or **F** (future) on the line.

_____1. Kim has left the keys in the car.

_____2. The car will have been stolen by the time we get back.

_____3. They have scolded her for her carelessness.

_____4. She had worked hard all summer to earn money for the car.

_____5. Kim has always been rather forgetful.

Copy each sentence, using the tense of the verb shown in parentheses.

1. Our club (collect, present perfect) one hundred model cars.

_____

2. Michelle (drive, present perfect) her first car.

_____

3. The new brakes (last, present perfect) all winter.

_____

4. She (save, past perfect) all year to buy a convertible.

_____

5. Mandy (buy, future tense) the car by the time we see her.

_____

Name _____

Water World

> The **progressive tense** of a verb shows action that is in progress. The present progressive tense shows action that is going on now. It is formed by adding a present tense form of be (am, is, are) to the present participle (-ing).
>
> *I am diving into the pool.*
>
> The past progressive tense shows action that was in progress in the past. It is formed by adding a past tense form of be (was or were) to the present participle (-ing).
>
> *I was planning to swim.*
>
> **Note:** The present participle is formed by adding -ing to the present tense of a verb. If a verb ends in a silent *e* (advise), the *e* is usually dropped (advising). If a one-syllable verb ends in a single vowel followed by a single consonant (cut), the final consonant is often doubled (cutting).

Underline the verb and write whether it is in the present or past progressive tense.

1. We were racing for the championship. _____

2. My parents are watching from the bleachers. _____

3. The relay race was taking the most time. _____

4. You are swimming the fastest. _____

5. I am floating in the ocean. _____

6. The synchronized swimmers were moving elegantly. _____

7. Swimming is becoming my favorite activity. _____

8. The team was winning. _____

9. I am starting my dive. _____

10. My pool toys are floating away. _____

Write five original sentences using the verb and the progressive tense shown in parentheses.

1. (run, past progressive) _____

2. (speak, past progressive) _____

3. (go, present progressive) _____

4. (paint, past progressive) _____

5. (chew, present progressive) _____

Name _____

Dear Diary

A **pronoun** is a word that takes the place of a noun. Personal pronouns indicate the speaker (first person), the one spoken to (second person), or the one spoken about (third person).

Singular	Plural
I, me, my, mine	we, us, our, ours
you, your, yours	you, your, yours
he, him, his, she her, hers, it, its	they, them, their, theirs

Circle the personal pronouns in the following diary entry.

Dear Diary,

You will never believe the day I had today! Our team played against the best soccer team in the

state in the tournament game. Everyone on their team was big and fast. They have been

undefeated all season, but so have we. When we started to play, I was pretty nervous. It turned

out to be a great game! My best friend, Joe, was our goalie, and he played really well. Only one

ball got past him. His foot slipped and he just couldn't stop it. Sam, my other friend, scored the

final goal. She was totally excited since it was her first goal of the entire season. Wow, what a

game for us. We beat them 5–1, and now the championship trophy is all ours!

Name _____

Together at Last

> **Contractions** are formed by combining two words.
> An apostrophe takes the place of letters that have been left out.
>   *I + am = I'm*

Write the contraction for each pair of words below.

1. we + had = _____
2. they + are = _____
3. it + is = _____
4. he + has = _____
5. they + have = _____
6. you + are = _____
7. it + will = _____
8. she + is = _____

9. we + are = _____
10. they + will = _____
11. I + have = _____
12. they + are = _____
13. I + will = _____
14. it + will = _____
15. she + has = _____
16. you + have = _____

In each sentence below, replace the underlined words with the correct contraction and write it on the line following the sentence.

1. <u>I have</u> always wanted to meet you. _____
2. I think <u>they will</u> go to school together. _____
3. <u>She would</u> like to have a best friend. _____
4. <u>We are</u> going to buy a tandem bike. _____
5. Please don't tell me <u>you have</u> decided to leave. _____
6. <u>He has</u> found his soulmate. _____
7. <u>It is</u> a bicycle with two seats. _____
8. <u>We will</u> always be friends. _____
9. <u>They have</u> been married for fifty years. _____
10. <u>I am</u> waiting for the woman of my dreams. _____

Name _____

Emergency Preparations

> A **subject pronoun** replaces a subject noun in a sentence.
> *Marybeth* closed the windows before the storm.
> *She* closed the windows before the storm.

In each of the following sentences, underline the subject noun. Then, rewrite the sentence and replace the subject noun with a subject pronoun.

1. A storm was coming to the little town soon.

   _____

2. Maxwell searched for a flashlight and batteries.

   _____

3. Cameron found the battery-operated radio.

   _____

4. Maxwell and Cameron took cover in the basement.

   _____

5. Fortunately, a stash of pillows and blankets was nearby.

   _____

6. Candles, matches, and jugs of fresh water were stored in a box under the bench too.

   _____

   _____

7. The boys could hear the wind whipping.

   _____

8. Lightning flashed outside the basement window.

   _____

Name _____

Classroom Clean-up

An **object pronoun** replaces the object of a sentence. The direct object tells what or whom receives the action of the verb.

*Mrs. Ophoff's class cleaned **the room** well.*
*Mrs. Ophoff's class cleaned **it** well.*

In each of the following sentences, cross out the direct object and replace it with an appropriate pronoun.

1. Toby sharpened the pencils.

2. Kate helped Susie and Tina hang up art projects.

3. Mrs. Ophoff cleaned the erasers outside.

4. Some girls helped Mrs. Ophoff by passing out the papers.

5. Paula won the prize for the cleanest desk.

6. Lucas washed the blackboard with water.

7. Stephen offered to help Lucas.

8. Jeffrey straightened all the books on the bookshelf.

9. Jim and Betsy emptied the trash cans.

10. Jason and Sharon fed the hamster.

11. DeShawn watered the plants.

12. Janie washed the tops of the desks.

13. Raquel put away the math game.

14. Carlos and Sonja cleaned out the lockers.

15. Chin swept the floor.

16. Manuel washed the windows.

IF87132 *Grammar*

Name _____

A Trampoline Tale

> **Singular pronouns** replace singular nouns, and **plural pronouns** replace plural nouns.
>
> *singular:* **She** *did flips on the trampoline.*
> *plural:* **They** *jumped on the trampoline.*

Underline each pronoun in the following story. Write **S** over the pronoun if it is singular; write **P** over the pronoun if it is plural.

My friends and I like to jump on the trampoline. My parents bought it for me and my sister for our birthdays. It is in the corner of our backyard in the shade. We usually take turns practicing flips and jumps. Dan and Rebekah like to jump with me. They have been working on their flips. Dan can do a high single flip, but he can't beat Rebekah. She is able to do a double flip without any trouble. I don't mean to boast, but I can top both of them. My specialty is a little more complicated. It is a backward double flip! Rebekah told me that she is going to practice her back flips today. Dan said he doesn't even want to try back flips. It is going to be a great day of fun for us.

List each different singular and plural pronoun you found.

SINGULAR		PLURAL
_____	_____	_____
_____	_____	_____
_____	_____	_____
		_____
		_____

Write the correct pronoun (singular or plural) to replace the underlined word on the line after each sentence.

1. David and I love to jump on <u>the trampoline</u>. _____
2. <u>The trampoline</u> was given as a gift. _____
3. Janie gave the tramp to <u>me and Rebekah</u>. _____
4. <u>Maurice</u> can do a double back flip with a twist. _____
5. Don't try to get <u>Mom and Dad</u> to jump. _____
6. <u>Tania</u> likes to show off for her friends. _____

Name _____

A Word from Our Sponsors

An **antecedent** is a word for which a pronoun stands. Use singular pronouns with singular antecedents and plural pronouns with plural antecedents.

*A good advertisement will sell **its** product. (singular)*
*Many companies advertise **their** products on T.V. (plural)*

In each of the following advertisements, underline the pronoun and draw an arrow to the antecedent.

Tuffy's Taffy stretches long and it tastes great!

Feed your puppy Perfect Pup food and he will be a perfectly healthy puppy.

Jackie's Life is now playing at theaters near you, and everyone will want to experience its magic.

Try Tony's Temporary Tattoos; they are easy to use and lots of fun for everyone.

Reach Sports Gear makes quality gear for all athletes wishing to reach their goals.

Famous supermodel, Sandra A. Mazing, wears Glossy Lips lipgloss because she knows a beautiful smile is important.

Buy a pack of Carver's tasty dry-roasted peanuts; you'll love them!

Pete's Party Pizza will make your party last on and on because no one can stop eating it.

Name _____

My Friend and Me

> A **verb** must agree with the **pronoun** in the subject part of the sentence.
> *He **runs**.* (singular)
> *They **run**.* (plural)

In each of the following sentences, circle the verb that agrees with the subject pronoun.

1. I (like, likes) my best friend a lot, but we (enjoy, enjoys) different things.

2. For instance, after school I (prefer, prefers) to have a snack and watch T.V., but he always (shoot, shoots) hoops in the driveway.

3. On Saturday morning, all the neighbor kids and I (meet, meets) to play soccer, but my friend (sleep, sleeps) in late.

4. Most people, including myself, love pizza, but he (hate, hates) it.

5. I ask him, "Why do you (wear, wears) that weird hat?"

6. He just (ignore, ignores) me.

7. We (know, knows) it doesn't matter that we're so different because we (is, are) best friends.

Write a sentence for each of these pronouns. Use each pronoun as the subject of the sentence and make sure the verb agrees with it.

(he)   1. _____

(it)   2. _____

(they)   3. _____

(we)   4. _____

(she)   5. _____

(you)   6. _____

Name _____

Baby Sitters at Your Service

Do not use an object pronoun as the subject of a sentence.

In a sentence with a compound subject, it is incorrect to put the pronoun *I* before the noun.

> *Me is glad you are here. (incorrect)*
> *I am glad you are here. (correct)*
> *Me and Jake play softball. (incorrect)*
> *Jake and I play softball. (correct)*

In each of the following sentences, circle the correct word or pair of words in the parentheses.

1. (Me, I) can baby-sit for you.

2. My friends and (me, I) took a baby-sitting course last summer.

3. The projects we did were very helpful for (me, I).

4. (I, me) made a baby-sitting kit to bring to your home.

5. Your kids and (me, I) will read books and play games together.

6. You can count on (me, I) to be responsible and trustworthy.

7. If you would like references, (me, I) can provide them.

8. (Me, I) believe I will do a wonderful job.

9. (I and you, You and I) can baby-sit together.

10. The money could be divided between (me and you, you and me).

11. (The children and I, I and the children) would like your help.

12. (You and I, You and me) would make a great baby-sitting team!

pronoun homophones

Let It Snow!

Pronoun homophones are pronouns that sound the same as other words but have different spellings and meanings and function differently in sentences.

These are possessive pronouns: *its, their, your, whose*

These are contractions: *it's, they're, you're, who's*

> **contraction: It's** *a beautiful day!*
> **pronoun: Its** *beauty comes from the bright sunshine.*

Circle the correct pronoun homophone in each of the following sentences.

1. (Its, It's) beginning to snow again.

2. (Whose, Who's) going sledding with me today?

3. Is (your, you're) new sled out in the barn?

4. (You're, Your) going to have to wear Grandpa's big boots.

5. I think (their, they're) on the back porch.

6. (Whose, Who's) stocking cap is this?

7. I really like (its, it's) fringy tassel.

8. I'm sure Grandma and Grandpa won't mind if we wear (their, they're) ski pants.

9. Hurry up, (its, it's) going to be dark outside by the time (your, you're) ready.

10. Grab (your, you're) gloves and let's go!

11. We've got to find the sleds. (Their, They're) probably hanging in Grandpa's barn.

12. (Whose, Who's) that sledding down the hill now?

13. It looks like David and Meagan with (their, they're) little brother.

14. This hill is perfect for sledding, and (its, it's) blanket of snow will provide a nice soft ride.

15. Let's race down the hill and see (whose, who's) sled is the fastest.

16. (Their, There) is little doubt that we will be faster.

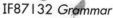

Name _____

Beach or Bust!

A **possessive pronoun** is one which indicates ownership or possession.
Possessive pronouns include: **my**, **mine**, **your**, **yours**, **his**, **her**, **hers**, **its**,
our, **ours**, **their**, **theirs**.

My family loves the beach.

In the following sentences, circle the possessive pronoun and underline the noun it modifies.

1. Look at all our stuff.

2. We will never get our things into the car.

3. My umbrella is far too large.

4. Your in-line skates will not fit in the front seat.

5. Is that surfboard his?

6. Put his board on top of the car.

7. You should put our cooler in the backseat.

8. What if there's not enough room for our bottles of pop?

9. Please don't smash my peanut butter and jelly sandwiches.

10. Her bicycle will have to stay behind.

11. I have already packed their beach bags.

12. Don't forget their folding chairs.

13. Make sure you pack the grill with its charcoal.

14. That beach blanket is mine.

15. Remember to bring your suntan lotion.

16. I'm going to bring my marshmallows.

17. Don't forget your graham crackers and chocolate bars.

18. My friends will bring their matches.

49

Name _____

The Five W's

An **interrogative pronoun** is used to begin a question.
Interrogative pronouns include: **who, whom, whose, what,** and **which.**
Who *is that masked man?*

Circle the interrogative pronouns in each of the following sentences. Then write answers for each of the questions.

1. Who is your hero?_____

2. What makes him (or her) so special to you?_____

3. Which quality about him (or her) do you admire most?_____

4. With whom do you spend a lot of your time?_____

5. Whose opinion means the most to you?_____

Fill in the blank with the most appropriate interrogative pronoun.

1. For _____ were these brownies made?

2. _____ kind are they?

3. _____ ate some of the frosting?

4. _____ one do you want?

5. _____ brownies are these anyway?

WHO MADE THESE SUPER BROWNIES?

Write your own questions using the interrogative pronouns below.

(who)   1. _____

(what)   2. _____

(whose) 3. _____

(which) 4. _____

(whom)   5. _____

Name _____

Who?

> **Who** is used as the subject of a verb and **whom** is used as the object. **Who's** is the contraction for *who is* and **whose** is a possessive pronoun.
>
> *Who was that masked man?*
> *You are waiting for whom?*
> *Who's making lunch for us today?*
> *Whose sandwich is this?*

In each of the following sentences, circle the correct word.

1. (Who's, Whose) on the phone?

2. To (who, whom) are you sending the package?

3. (Who's, Whose) sticky mess is this?

4. For (who, whom) is he waiting?

5. (Who, Whom) ate the last meatball?

6. I have been wondering (who's, whose) stinky socks these are.

7. Do you know (who, whom) is having a birthday today?

8. The cat of (who, whom) we speak is named Lola.

9. (Who's, Whose) yellow raincoat are you wearing?

10. We've been waiting all day to find out (who, whom) the winner is.

11. I appreciate my sister, to (who, whom) I tell all my secrets.

12. The author, (who's, whose) book you are reading, will sign autographs this afternoon.

13. (Who, Whom) would like a hot fudge sundae?

14. For (who, whom) did you sing that love song?

15. Can you remember (who, whom) won the Stanley Cup in 1998?

16. We met a man (who's, whose) hair was bright green!

Name _____

We Love a Parade

> An **indefinite pronoun** is one which gives an approximate number or quantity. It does not tell exactly how many or how much. Some indefinite pronouns include *many, more, fewer, some, several, all,* and *each.* These pronouns often act as adjectives.
>
> *The big parade enticed many people downtown.*

Circle each indefinite pronoun in the sentences below.

1. Many people line the streets to watch the parade.

2. Once the parade begins, several marching bands perform for the crowd.

3. Each band member marches to the cadence of the drum.

4. Usually, a few clowns ride their unicycles.

5. All of the children stand close to the street to get a closer look.

6. Some people in the parade toss candy to the children.

7. The big kids often catch more candy than the little ones.

8. A few fire trucks join in the fun.

9. It seems that every year there are more floats than the year before.

10. The parade is great fun for each person who participates.

11. Anyone can join in the fun.

12. Both children and adults work to creat floats.

13. When work is going on, most people are enthusiastic.

14. A few happy people make the whole crew work better.

Name _____

For Me?

A **reflexive pronoun** reflects the action of the verb back to the subject.		
	singular	plural
first	myself	ourselves
second	yourself	yourselves
third	herself, himself, itself	themselves

The winners congratulated themselves.

Underline the reflexive pronoun in each sentence. Then, circle the noun or pronoun to which the reflexive pronoun refers.

1. The children treated themselves to ice cream.
2. They timed themselves during the race.
3. Mary dressed herself for school.
4. We introduced ourselves to the new student.
5. Did you make this yourself?

If the reflexive pronoun in each sentence below is used incorrectly, circle it and write the correct reflexive pronoun on the line. If the sentence is correct, write **correct**.

1. I told myself it must be a lie. _____
2. We reminded ourself of the time. _____
3. Did she blame herselves for the accident? _____
4. Some artists have painted theirselves. _____
5. She bought herself a new dress. _____
6. The naughty dog helped itself to some apple pie. _____
7. He asked hisself what to do. _____
8. Did you take that piece of cake for yourselves, David? _____
9. Please control yourself. _____
10. Betsy and Sara took theirselves out to a movie. _____

 adjectives

Name _____

Piles of Puckering Pickles

Adjectives are words that describe nouns.
The *fuzzy little* bumblebee buzzed about the *fragrant* flowers.

Circle all the adjectives in the pickle advertisement. Write ten more adjectives, one in each pickle.

COOL
and
CRUNCHY
GARLIC
DILL PICKLES

The world's tastiest garlic pickles
for the
world's coolest, hungriest kids.

These crispy and zesty snacks
are the best for
crunching and munching.

BITE-SIZED TREATS TO TICKLE
YOUR TIRED TASTEBUDS

IF87132 *Grammar*

Name _____

That's Corny

> An **adjective** modifies a noun or pronoun. It gives specific
> information by telling *what kind, how many,* or *which one.*
>
> *purple* cow
> *thirteen* footprints
> *that* creep

In each of the following sentences, circle the adjectives.

1. Tall cornstalks grow during the hot summer months.

2. That Indian corn is extremely colorful.

3. We like to pop yellow corn because it puffs up big and fluffy.

4. Some people like to eat caramel corn, but I don't.

5. Sometimes Mom cooks one jumbo-sized can of creamed corn for Sunday dinner.

6. Still, I prefer juicy corn on the cob.

7. In art class, we made these corn husk dolls.

8. Corn was first used by North and South Americans.

9. Grandma bakes fluffy cornbread whenever she serves her spicy Texan chili.

10. A fat and crispy corndog is the perfect treat at the county fair.

11. Cows munch on dry corn at mealtimes.

12. Most corn is grown in the prolific Corn Belt of the United States.

Write three original sentences using the adjectives given.

1. (green) _____

   _____

2. (those) _____

   _____

3. (rusty) _____

   _____

55

adjectives

Name _____

Forty Feathered Falcons

An **adjective** modifies a noun or pronoun. It gives specific information by telling *what kind, how many*, or *which one*.

    yellow buttercup
    forty ferrets
    that thorn

In front of each adjective–noun pair, write **1** for *what kind*, **2** for *how many*, or **3** for *which one*.

_____ two teaspoons

_____ poor pilot

_____ nine nuns

_____ that man

_____ blue balloon

_____ eighty eggs

_____ brown bear

_____ strong sailor

_____ fast footwork

_____ this week

_____ mean muskrat

_____ one wish

_____ frantic Fred

_____ pink posies

_____ growing garden

_____ jade jewelry

_____ opposite opinions

_____ these things

_____ four friends

_____ some sneakers

_____ an apple

_____ crazy clowns

_____ vivacious Vivian

_____ those thugs

Name _____

Take Me Out to the Ballgame

> *A*, *an*, and *the* are the three most commonly used **articles**. *A* and *an* are **indefinite articles**, referring to any one of a class of nouns. *A* is used before words that begin with consonants. Use *an* before words that begin with vowels. *The* is **definite** and refers to a specific noun.
>
> **a** *shower*
> **an** *apple*
> **the** *dog*

Use either *a*, *an*, or *the* to complete the sentences below.

Baseball is _____ All-American sport. It is played with _____ leather-covered ball and _____ wooden or metal bat. _____ batter swings and hits _____ ball across _____ diamond-shaped field. Then he begins to run _____ bases. If he is able to run all _____ way back to home plate, where he started, he has scored _____ homerun. _____ outfielder or _____ infielder tries to catch _____ ball and stop _____ runner. In _____ inning, each team is allowed three *outs*. _____ game is finished at _____ end of nine innings.

Circle the correct article in each sentence below.

1. Everyone has to have (a, an) hotdog.

2. Many people try to catch (a, an) homerun ball.

3. Most root for (a, the) home team and hope for (a, an) win.

4. (A, An) umpire calls balls and strikes from behind (a, the) catcher.

5. I like to sing (a, an) enthusiastic round of "Take Me Out to the Ballgame."

6. Before we leave, we always try to get (a, an) autograph from at least one player.

proper adjectives

Name _____

Around the World

Proper nouns are the specific names of people, places, or things. **Proper adjectives** are formed from these proper nouns. They usually begin with capital letters.

North American people
Canadian bacon

Underline all of the adjectives. Write a **P** above the proper adjectives and a **C** above the common (regular) ones.

Italian spaghetti	hot cocoa	green shamrocks	Polish sausage
Swiss chocolate	fun fiesta	wooden shoes	sausage meatballs
sumo wrestling	Irish pub	Mexican border	Japanese kimono
African safari	Dutch dance	tall giraffes	Spanish rice
friendly dog	flour tortillas	lively polka	English setter

In the following sentences, capitalize the proper adjectives.

1. On Saturday mornings, we usually have french toast.

2. Mom always buys idaho potatoes at the supermarket.

3. For my birthday, I had chinese food and chocolate cake.

4. Dad's spicy texan chili is great on a cold day.

5. The restaurant on the corner serves a great greek salad with anchovies.

6. I love to eat maine lobster dipped in melted butter.

7. Grandma's german potato salad is too sour for my taste.

8. Her belgian waffles are heavenly, though.

9. We enjoy spicy latin american foods.

10. One of the best desserts in the world is new york cheesecake.

Name _____

Rocky, the Wonder Dog

> There are three forms, or degrees, of adjectives that are used in comparison. The **positive** degree is used to describe one item or person. The **comparative** degree is used when making a comparison between two items or people. The **superlative** degree is used when comparing more than two items or people.
>
> *positive:* George is crafty.
> *comparative:* George is craftier than Roger.
> *superlative:* George is the craftiest of the three boys.

Complete the adjective chart.

POSITIVE	COMPARATIVE	SUPERLATIVE
loud	_____	_____
quick	_____	_____
tardy	_____	_____
stinky	_____	_____
wise	_____	_____
sweet	_____	_____
angry	_____	_____
bright	_____	_____
strong	_____	_____
green	_____	_____

In the following sentences, underline the comparative and superlative adjectives. If the adjective is comparative, write **C** in the blank. If it is superlative, write **S**.

_____ 1. Rocky is the coolest dog around.

_____ 2. He has a few white spots on his ears and a bigger spot on his nose.

_____ 3. Rocky is the strongest member of my family.

_____ 4. He is the loudest sleeper in my family.

_____ 5. My dog has a louder snore than I do.

_____ 6. His coat is softer than any of my aunt's dogs.

_____ 7. Rocky is a better frisbee catcher than anyone I know.

_____ 8. He is also the highest jumper.

_____ 9. And, he is the fastest runner of all my pets.

_____ 10. Rocky is the smartest dog in the world.

Name _____

Sammy

> **Adjectives** change form to show comparison. The endings **er** and **est** are added, or comparison words such as *more, most, less,* and *least* are used. Do not use comparison words with **er** or **est** words.
>
> *Sammy is my most specialest cousin. (incorrect)*
> *Sammy is my most special cousin. (correct)*
> *He is more friendlier than anyone I know. (incorrect)*
> *He is friendlier than anyone I know. (correct)*

Circle the correct adjective in each of the following sentences.

1. My cousin Sammy is the (cutest, most cutest) kid!

2. He's only three years old, and he does the (funnier, funniest) things.

3. Sammy is (more fun, most fun) than any other little kids I know.

4. When I push him on the swings he always says, "Push me (faster, more faster), Bailey!"

5. When we play on the merry-go-round, we go (slower, slowest) than the big kids.

6. Usually, I carry him home on my back because it's (quicker, quickest) than having him walk.

7. He says the (craziest, most craziest) things, too.

8. Besides that, Sammy always tells me that I am his (smartest, most smart) cousin.

9. Sammy's hair is even (redder, more redder) than mine.

10. His dimples are the (bigger, biggest) I have ever seen.

11. He has the (most adorable, most adorablest) smile in the whole world.

12. The time we spend together is (more special, most special) to me than just about anything.

13. The day we spend together is (more better, better) than the other days of the week.

14. The time I spend with my other cousins in the (worst, worstest).

Name _____

At the Movies

> *This, that, these,* and *those* are **demonstrative adjectives** that point out a particular person, place, or thing. Use *this* and *these* for things close by and *that* and *those* for things distant in time or space. *This* and *that* are singular. *These* and *those* are plural.
>
> **this** *box at my feet*   **these** *boxes at my feet*
>
> **that** *box in the other*   **those** *boxes in the*
>   *room*   *other room*

Circle the most appropriate demonstrative adjective in each sentence below.

1. (These, Those) tickets cost less than the ones for the evening show.

2. Let's get some of (this, that) popcorn over there.

3. I like (this, that) theater better than the one across town.

4. Grab two of (these, those) seats down in front.

5. (This, That) screen might actually be too close now.

6. Let's move back to (these, those) seats behind us.

7. (This, That) movie is pretty good.

8. And (these, those) seats are better, aren't they?

Write a demonstrative adjective before each of the following objects.

_____ papers (near)   _____ dog (far)

_____ globe (far)   _____ rollercoaster (near)

_____ hand (near)   _____ shoes (far)

_____ hair style (far)   _____ dentures (near)

_____ candy (near)   _____ students (far)

_____ athletes (far)   _____ football field (near)

_____ city (near)   _____ goat (far)

_____ mall (far)   _____ movie stars (near)

  IF87132 *Grammar*

Name _____

A Good Job Well Done

> **Good** and **bad** are adjectives. **Well** and **badly** are adverbs.
> *Matthew made a **good** shot.*
> *A **bad** pass messed up the play.*
> *Matthew played **well**.*
> *The ball was passed **badly**.*

In each of the following sentences, circle the correct modifier in the parentheses.

1. Miko is a (good, well) artist.

2. She paints nature scenes especially (good, well).

3. She doesn't do too (bad, badly) on portraits either.

4. Her paintings of the ocean at sunrise are really (good, well).

5. Miko says she paints (good, well) when she is outside.

6. I would like to paint as (good, well) as she.

1. Stanley plays the guitar (good, well).

2. I must admit that I play the guitar very (bad, badly).

3. He has a (good, well) guitar too.

4. The music he writes is (good, well).

5. His lyrics aren't (bad, badly) written.

6. Unfortunately, his voice isn't very (good, well).

1. I try not to get (bad, badly) grades.

2. Right now I am doing pretty (good, well) in writing.

3. I had (good, well) comments on my last story.

4. I know I can write better if I practice (good, well).

5. I think I will do (well, good) on my next paper.

6. If I do (bad, badly), I may have to spend less time playing.

Name _____

The Toothache

> An **adverb** is a word that modifies a verb, an adjective, or another adverb. Adverbs indicate *time*, *place*, or *manner*.
>
> **time:** *brushes daily*
> **place:** *flosses here*
> **manner:** *gargles noisily*

In the following sentences, circle the adverbs and indicate if they are time **(T)**, place **(P)**, or manner **(M)**.

_____ 1. My tooth ached badly.

_____ 2. Mom immediately decided that I had to go to the dentist.

_____ 3. Before I knew it, I was waiting there in Dr. Chang's office.

_____ 4. The nauseating smell of antiseptic really bothered me.

_____ 5. I tapped my fingers anxiously on the chair.

_____ 6. I now noticed a man had fallen asleep while he waited for the dentist.

_____ 7. A woman across the room silently read a magazine.

_____ 8. Finally, the nurse called my name.

_____ 9. I stood and walked in.

_____10. At that moment, I felt nauseatingly sick to my stomach.

_____11. Soon the nurse directed me to a dental chair.

_____12. Instantly, the dentist arrived wearing a mask and plastic gloves.

_____13. He was smiling broadly behind his mask.

_____14. "Let's take a look here," he said.

_____15. I sat there hoping he would not yank out my tooth.

_____16. I always dread going to that dentist's chair.

Name _____

Late Kate

> An adverb is a word that modifies a verb, an adjective, or another adverb. **Adverbs of time** answer the questions *when* or *how often*.
>
> *We like to go to the movies* **sometimes**.

Use the adverbs of time from the Word Bank to modify the verbs and complete the sentences below. **Note:** You will not use all the words in the bank.

Word Bank

never	eventually	next	usually	often
then	frequently	first	always	finally
later	soon	seldom	today	constantly

Late Kate was _ _ _ _ _ _ on time for anything. _ _ _ _ _ _ _ _ she was very late for everything. Kate _ _ _ _ _ _ arrived at school after the tardy bell had rung. _ _ _ _ _ _ _ _ _ _ _ she made her friends wait for her. "Hurry, hurry, slow-poke Kate," they _ _ _ _ _ _ _ said.

_ _ _ _ _ _ _ _ _ _ _ Kate's friends had waited long enough. _ _ _ _ _ _ they decided to teach her a lesson that they hoped she would never forget. _ _ _ _ _ _ _ Kate's friends sent her an invitation to a special party given in her honor. They set to work, and _ _ _ _ _ the room was decorated with streamers and bright colored balloons. _ _ _ _ _ _ _ _ _ they hung a banner from one end of the room to the next. _ _ _ _ _ all of Kate's friends went home. Sure enough, Kate arrived _ _ _ _ _ _, but she was sad to discover only a quiet room and a banner that read "Sorry you are late Kate. You missed all the fun!"

Use the three adverbs from the Word Bank that were not used in the above sentences to write sentences of your own. Be sure the adverb modifies a verb.

1. _____

2. _____

3. _____

Name _____

A Cinderella Story

> **Adverbs of place** answer the question *where*. They usually modify verbs.
> *Cinderella's stepsisters were always **nearby** with work for her to do.*

In the following sentences, circle the adverbs that answer the question *where* and underline the verbs they modify.

1. Cinderella was sent upstairs to live in the attic.

2. Mice lived there too.

3. Spiderwebs hung everywhere in her dismal room.

4. Sadness and gloom threatened inside.

5. But, the sun shone outside her window.

6. Cinderella's stepmother and stepsisters stayed downstairs.

7. Cinderella could come down only to cook and clean for them.

8. When they were away, she would sit beside the fire.

9. As the fire blazed, her mice friends searched nearby for some crumbs.

10. Here she could dream of faraway places and happy endings.

11. Cinderella longed to meet her prince at the ball and run away with him.

12. Her wonderful fairy godmother arranged to get Cinderella there.

13. And so, Cinderella ran away with her prince.

Fill in an adverb that answers *where* in each of the following sentences.

1. The sparkling carriage stopped _____ the castle.
2. Cinderella and the prince danced _____ a glittering chandelier.
3. They strolled _____ the twinkling stars.
4. The prince looked _____ for Cinderella.

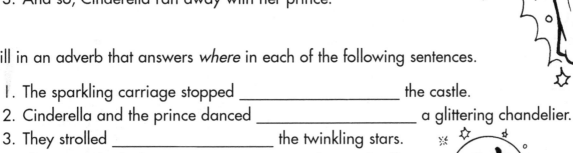

Name _____

The Pool Party

> **Adverbs of manner** answer the questions *how* or *in what manner*.
> They often end in *-ly*.
>
> *Put on your swimsuit **quickly**.*

In each of the following sentences, circle the adverb of manner and underline the verb it modifies.

1. Mr. Peter's fifth grade class rushed excitedly to the pool area.

2. The clear blue water sparkled invitingly in the sunshine.

3. Quickly everyone prepared to jump into the pool.

4. Suddenly Carlos yelled, "Wait everybody!"

5. "Let's all jump together," he continued.

6. Mr. Peters offered to count aloud to three and yell "Go."

7. All the students stood expectantly around the pool.

8. When everyone was ready, Mr. Peters loudly shouted, "1, 2, 3,...GO!"

9. Twenty-nine students leaped simultaneously into the cold pool water.

10. Together they created a huge burst of water.

11. Everyone hollered happily and splashed one another.

12. While they celebrated, Mr. Peters totally surprised them by doing an enormous cannonball off the diving board.

Fill in an adverb that answers *how* or *in what manner* in each of the following sentences.

1. Patrick _____ dove off the high board.
2. Mary Ann _____ stuck a toe into the cold pool water.
3. Chin ran _____ toward the pool and did a belly flop.
4. "Bombs away!" Chin yelled _____ .

Name _____

Positive, Comparative, Superlative

> There are three forms, or degrees, of **adverbs** that are used in comparison. The **positive degree** is used when describing one action. The **comparative degree** is used when comparing two actions. The **superlative degree** is used when comparing more than two actions. When an adverb ends in *ly*, it usually compares by adding *more* or *most*.
>
> | Positive | Comparative | Superlative |
> |---|---|---|
> | low | lower | lowest |
> | carefully | more carefully | most carefully |

Write the missing adverbs in the chart.

POSITIVE	COMPARATIVE	SUPERLATIVE
sweetly	more sweetly	
late		latest
quietly		
		soonest
clearly		
safely		
rapidly		
		hardest
high		
		most easily
	more quickly	
		most powerfully
deep		
gracefully		
tragically		
		most playfully

Name _____

'Round and About

> A **preposition** is a word that relates a noun or a pronoun to another word in the sentence. Prepositions indicate a relationship between separate things.
>
> My book bag is **near** the door.
> His shoes are **on** his feet.

Familiarize yourself with several prepositions by filling in the word search puzzle.
Look ↓ ↑ ← → ↗ ↙ . A few two-letter prepositions may appear more than once.

Word Bank

during	to	of	past	for	with
onto	by	through	beyond	beside	around
in	near	between	over	about	outside
until	from	since	off	after	below
under	before				

D	U	R	I	N	G	A	R	D	T	J
B	Y	O	N	T	O	W	U	R	H	O
E	E	M	E	C	K	O	V	E	R	U
T	C	P	A	S	T	F	U	T	O	T
W	N	A	R	B	Q	F	N	F	U	S
E	I	E	T	D	O	L	T	A	G	I
E	S	T	E	R	L	X	I	R	H	D
N	Q	V	H	I	B	E	L	O	W	E
J	B	E	S	I	D	E	N	S	R	M
Y	A	R	O	U	N	D	Y	G	E	O
H	D	K	G	H	X	P	L	O	D	R
B	E	F	O	R	E	M	I	S	N	F
Q	N	Z	C	A	B	O	U	T	U	D

Name _____

One Hump or Two?

> A **prepositional phrase** is a group of words that begins with a preposition and ends with the object of the preposition. A preposition is a word or group of words that shows a relationship between the words in a sentence.
>
> *There are several different kinds **of camels**.*

Underline each prepositional phrase in the following sentences.

1. Camels are animals that have humps on their backs.

2. A large lump of fat is located inside the hump.

3. A dromedary is a camel with just one hump.

4. Some animals without humps also belong to the camel family.

5. Many camels live in the African and Arabian deserts.

6. Others live in the South American mountains.

7. The camels' huge feet help them to walk over hot desert sand.

8. They have broad bony ridges above each eye to shield them from the sun.

9. A camel can shut its nostrils to keep sand out of its nose.

10. Camels have large eyes on the sides of their heads.

11. The camel's hump is a place for storing fat, but not water.

12. A thirsty camel can drink more than fifty gallons of water in one day.

13. Camels do not need to drink water during cooler weather.

14. A camel can travel long distances across hot deserts.

15. Today, camels are still used by nomads.

16. In desert areas, camels pull plows and turn water wheels to irrigate fields.

17. On extremely hot days, a camel keeps cool by resting in a shady place.

18. The long fur of some camels is good for weaving into cloth.

Name _____

Camp Cooleewowa

> The noun or pronoun used as the **object of the preposition** follows the preposition. The object and the preposition form what is called the **prepositional phrase**. Often, a prepositional phrase that begins a sentence will be set off by a comma.
>
> *Brett fell **in the stream**.*
> *It seemed very funny **to us**.*
> ***Instead of helping him**, we laughed and laughed.*
>
> To find the object of the preposition, ask *whom* or *what* after the preposition.
>
> *Brett fell in **what**? the stream*
> *It seemed funny to **whom**? us*
> *Instead of helping **whom**? him*

Read the paragraphs below. Place parentheses around the prepositional phrases and underline the object of the preposition.

Every summer I go with my best friend to Camp Cooleewowa. It's a really cool place. Ten campers and two counselors stay in each cabin. We put our sleeping bags on the bunk beds and slide our suitcases under the bottom bunk. There is a fireplace at one end of the room. Each night, we start a fire in the fireplace to warm the cabin before bedtime. Everything is perfect, except for the bathrooms; we use stinky outhouses!

The camp is located on the northern side of Lake Coolee. Every morning we get to go canoeing across the lake. In the afternoon, we dive off the docks into the crystal-clear lake water. After dinner, all the campers gather to play games like volleyball, basketball, and soccer. Before bedtime, everyone meets around the fire pit on the beach. The bright fire burning in the darkness gets us telling spooky stories and silly camp songs.

At the end of an exciting week, we all go home knowing that we will come back again next summer for another week of Cooleewowa fun.

Name _____

Fruity Flavors

> A prepositional phrase is a group of words that shows how two words or ideas are related to each other. Like a one-word adjective, an **adjective prepositional phrase** modifies a noun or pronoun.
>
> *My favorite fruit **in the whole world** is the orange.*

In the following sentences, underline the adjective prepositional phrases and circle the words being modified.

1. The peaches in the bowl will make a tasty pie.

2. The fruit stand near the corner has quarts of fresh raspberries for sale.

3. The cantaloupe in the refrigerator will be a good bedtime snack.

4. A handful of sliced grapes will sweeten the chicken salad.

5. The bananas on the trees are still not ripe.

6. A big watermelon from the garden will be our dessert.

7. The pineapples of the Hawaiian islands are sweet and juicy.

8. One cherry on top of an ice-cream sundae is just right.

9. One of the oranges next to the salad bowl was as big as a softball.

10. Let's pick the berries along the fence.

11. Pies with a lot of fruit are the best.

12. I love the blueberries from Grandpa's farm.

13. Bananas with very dark spots usually end up in banana bread.

14. The pears from our own pear trees are yellowish-green.

15. Most fruits of any season are flavorful.

Name _____

Bowl-a-thon

Like a one-word adverb, an **adverb prepositional phrase** usually modifies a verb and may tell *where, how,* or *when* an action takes place. It relates a word or phrase in a sentence to another word or phrase.

> *We went bowling **at the bowling alley**.*
> (where did we go bowling?)
> *We bowled **with our friends cheering us on**.*
> (how did we bowl?)
> *We went bowling **after school**.*
> (when did we go bowling?)

In each of the following sentences, underline the adverb prepositional phrase and circle the verb or verb phrase being modified.

Jason goes bowling on Saturday mornings.

He and his friends meet at 10:00 a.m.

They each choose a ball before starting.

The boys sit at the scoring table.

The girls bowl their first frames with enthusiasm.

Rosie usually rolls her ball into the gutter.

Everyone cheers and applauds from behind her.

Most of the time Jason bowls a few strikes.

They put a dollar in a cup for each strike.

A turkey is three strikes in a row.

Whoever bowls the first turkey keeps the money for himself.

Whoever wins the money gets to wear the turkey button on his shirt.

Jason and his friends have a great time at the bowling alley.

Name _____

Art in a Box

> A **prepositional phrase** contains a preposition and a noun or pronoun acting as the object of the preposition. These phrases can act as *adjectives* or *adverbs*.
>
> Follow the directions **on this page**.
> (adjective—describes which directions)
>
> Follow the directions **with care**.
> (adverb—describes how to follow)

In the following sentences, underline the prepositional phrases. On each line, write **ADJ** if it is an adjective phrase or **ADV** if it is an adverb phrase. Then complete the picture.

____1. Add hair to the stick person.

____2. Color the cat next to the person black.

____3. Draw a silver lining around each cloud.

____4. Put a flower on the middle stem.

____5. Sketch a bird flying between the clouds.

____6. Create green grass beneath the cat and the stick person.

____7. Put a butterfly net in the stick person's right hand.

____8. Make butterflies flying about the net.

____9. Give the flower at the far right a smiley face.

____10. Color the sky behind the scene light blue.

____11. Draw two eyes and a smile on the stick person's face.

____12. Add a tail to the cat's left side.

Name _____

Happy Trails

> Some words can be used as prepositions or as adverbs.
> An adverb will not have an object as a preposition does.
> **preposition:** *The wagon traveled **down** the mountain.*
> **adverb:** *The rain came **down** and soaked the wagon.*

Write **preposition** or **adverb** on the line to show the use of the underlined word in each sentence.

1. The horses weren't complaining <u>about</u> the wagons full of hayriders. _____

2. The trees seemed to smile as we passed <u>by</u>. _____

3. The hay kept us warm as we rode <u>beneath</u> the stars. _____

4. Stars seem to shine so brightly when city lights aren't <u>around</u>. _____

5. The sky stretched <u>above</u> as we sang hay-ride songs. _____

6. It felt great sitting <u>beside</u> the fire. _____

7. The horses pulled the wagons <u>along</u> the dusty trail. _____

8. The horses seemed thirsty as they waded <u>across</u> the stream. _____

9. I was a little frightened, but my horse went <u>through</u> just fine. _____

10. Traveling seems more peaceful when you leave your car <u>behind</u>. _____

Change the adverb to a preposition by completing each sentence below.

1. The wagon creaked <u>along</u> _____

2. We rode <u>past</u> _____

3. Falling stars streaked the sky <u>above</u> _____

4. Happy faces were all <u>around</u> _____

5. Darkness fell <u>outside</u> _____

6. We all gathered <u>around</u> _____

7. Everyone walked <u>along</u> _____

8. We went <u>inside</u> _____

9. The wagon went <u>down</u> _____

10. We all climbed <u>off</u> _____

Name _____

Gosh, Thanks

Interjections are words that express strong feeling or sudden emotion. An interjection may be followed by an exclamation point or a comma. Interjections are more effective when they are not overused.

Wow! What a surprise!
Oh, give me a break.

Choose an interjection from the Word Bank for each of the following sentences.

WORD BANK

wow	yikes	oh	oops
ouch	phew	eureka	hey
help	well	thanks	yes
ugh	psst	gosh	whew
aha	shh	nonsense	terrific

1. _____! I am glad you made the team.
2. _____! I can't lift this by myself.
3. _____, I think I get it now.
4. _____! Please be quiet!
5. _____! That was a close one.
6. _____! That never happened.
7. _____! I really made a mess.
8. _____, that was very nice of you
9. _____! We've caught you!
10. _____, would you like to come along with us?

Write sentences with the following interjections.

1. Wow! _____

2. Ouch! _____

3. Phew! _____

4. Eureka! _____

5. Well, _____

Name _____

Hockey

An **appositive** is a noun, pronoun, or noun phrase placed next to, or very near, another noun or pronoun to identify, explain, or rename it.

*Wayne Gretsky, **a famous hockey player**, retired from the New York Rangers in 1999.*

In each of the following sentences, underline the appositive and circle the noun it explains. Add commas around the appositives.

1. Hockey a popular sport is played in Canada, in the United States of America, and in Europe.

2. Fast-skating Sid a fair and friendly referee gives out penalties.

3. Frank drives the Zamboni an ice-smoothing machine around the rink.

4. Some players wear masks wire face guards to protect themselves.

5. Hockey players who are tough athletes train and practice daily.

6. Hockey may have developed from a game played by Neanderthals prehistoric humans.

7. Players who participate in fighting may have to spend time at the penalty bench or penalty box.

8. The goals net covered structures stand at each end of the ice.

9. A hat trick three goals scored by a single player in one game is a rarity.

10. Players spend time in the penalty box a glassed-in seating area after breaking the game's rules.

11. Hockey fans people of all ages cheer loudly for their favorite team.

12. Fighting a frequent occurrence may result in penalties or expulsion from the game.

13. Icing flinging the puck from one end of the rink to the other should be avoided.

14. Gordy Howe a famous hockey player played for the Redwings.

15. Before the 1870's, a rubber ball rather than a puck was used to play hockey.

16. Clarence the hockey goalie loves to stop the puck.

17. The NHL teams compete for the ultimate reward the Stanley Cup.

18. The first professional hockey team was organized in 1903 in Michigan the home of the Detroit Redwings.

double negatives

Name _____

Enter at Your Own Risk

Use only one negative when you mean to say *no.*

It **doesn't** do **no** good to clean your room if you just get it messy again. *(incorrect)*

It **doesn't** do any good to clean your room if you just get it messy again. *(correct)*

Circle the correct word from the pair in parentheses.

1. I can't (ever, never) keep my room clean for very long.

2. I recommend that you don't (ever, never) enter my room when it is a mess.

3. There isn't (any, no) way out of such a disaster area.

4. In fact, you might not (ever, never) escape.

5. There just aren't (any, no) guarantees for your safety.

Enter at Your Own Risk!!!

6. In fact, we haven't been able to find (anyone, no one) who entered last week.

7. There isn't a sign of them (anywhere, nowhere).

8. Besides that, I haven't (ever, never) found my pet snake in there either.

9. She wasn't (anywhere, nowhere) to be seen.

10. Believe me, it doesn't make (any, no) sense to go in there if you don't have to.

Correct the double negatives in these sentences.

1. We won't do none of your cleaning for you.

_____

2. I don't want no money to help you clean it.

_____

3. I'm sorry, but I can't do nothing to help you out.

_____

4. There isn't nobody here who will clean your room.

_____

5. The maid came, but there wasn't nobody home.

_____

6. There weren't no window cleaner left.

_____

Name _____

Oops!

A **sentence** is a group of words that expresses a complete thought.
Sentences must have subjects and predicates. The subject tells whom
or what the sentence is about. The predicate tells what the subject is
or does.

> *Emily runs out of school.* (sentence)
> *Yells at her little brother.* (not a sentence)

Put a star next to each group of words below that is a sentence.

1. The school bell rang.
2. Running out of school.
3. Slipped on a banana peel.
4. Jeff fell on the ground.
5. His knee was cut.

Draw a vertical line between the subject and the predicate in each sentence below.

1. Shawn clumsily tripped over a garden rake.
2. The little girl tumbled down the basement stairs.
3. My dad bumped his head on the chandelier.
4. The dog skid on the rug and hit the wall.
5. Melissa slid on a leaf and fell while in-line skating.

Add words to the groups of words below to make them into complete sentences. Make as many
different sentences as you can.

- the exhausted backpackers
- deserted in the mountains
- a scary noise

_____

_____

_____

_____

_____

_____

_____

_____

_____

Name _____

Ice Cream, You Scream!

> The **simple subject** is the essential noun of the sentence, not including articles or modifiers. It cannot be left out of a complete subject.
>
> *The **team** won free ice-cream cones.*

In each of the following sentences, draw a box around the simple subject.

1. Ice cream tastes great on a hot day.

2. Most people enjoy at least one kind of ice cream.

3. After the soccer game, we went to Cone World for an ice-cream treat.

4. My choice is always the same.

5. I choose chocolate every time.

6. Karla hates chocolate.

7. She gets one dip of bubblegum and one dip of blue moon.

8. Kyle says that is gross!

9. Kyle's favorite is a banana split with a cherry on the top.

10. Once in a while, our coach buys us ice cream.

11. The team always plays better if the ice cream is going to be free.

12. Today we won the playoffs.

13. Our coach bought us jumbo banana splits.

14. Kyle ate so much he says he will never even look at another banana split.

15. Karla got in a food fight with Jack.

16. I hid under a table.

17. The coach told Karla and Jack to help mop the floor.

Name _____

Grandma Mae

> The **complete subject** of a sentence is the noun, pronoun, or group of words acting as a noun that tells who or what the sentence is about. Complete subjects include modifiers such as adjectives or prepositions.
>
> ***My sweet grandmother*** *knitted a sweater.*

Underline the complete subject in each sentence below.

1. My grandma has her own way of doing things.

2. When we go out, she always carries an umbrella.

3. Her hot pink suede shoes are the coolest.

4. Grandma Mae never leaves the house without a hat either.

5. One of her favorite hats has a big floppy brim trimmed with plastic pansies.

6. All of her fingers display huge rings, which Grandma calls her "baubles."

7. Once a month, a hair dresser dyes Grandma Mae's hair purple.

8. I think her hair complements her pink suede shoes nicely.

9. Most of the time, her pet Chihuahua sits in Grandma's big straw purse.

10. Grandma calls her dog Kisses.

11. When we eat at Grandma's house, she makes all our meals into works of art.

12. For dessert, she carves birds out of apples.

13. My mom and dad say Grandma is eccentric.

14. I believe Grandma Mae is the best grandma in the world.

Name _____

A Snowy Home

> The **simple predicate** is the verb or verb phrase that tells what the subject is or what it does. It does not include any modifying words. The simple predicate cannot be left out of the complete predicate.
>
> *Eskimos* **create** *dome-shaped homes out of snow blocks.*

In each of the following sentences, draw a box around the simple predicate.

1. Jamie and Dad built an igloo in their backyard.

2. They made the bricks out of snow.

3. After a few hours, the igloo was finished.

4. The snow fell all day long.

5. Dad suggested something adventurous.

6. Dad and Jamie agreed to spend the night in their igloo.

7. Dad cooked beans on the campstove.

8. Jamie poured hot chocolate into mugs.

9. After dinner, Dad told Jamie ghost stories.

10. Before dark, Jamie laid the sleeping bags on top of a blanket inside the igloo.

11. Dad grabbed the flashlights and pillows.

12. At bedtime, they snuggled into their sleeping bags.

13. Of course, Mom worried about them.

14. Still, the winter campers stayed warm all night long in their igloo.

15. They had a great time too.

Name _____

Twice as Nice

> The **complete predicate** is the verb or verb phrase, containing all modifiers, that tells what the subject is or what it does.
>
> *The twins, Clay and Carla Crawford,* **were born on July 4, 1990.**

In each of the following sentences, underline the complete predicate.

1. My sister and I are twins.

2. Her name is Carla Marie Crawford.

3. My full name is Clayton Maxwell Crawford.

4. Everyone calls me Clay.

5. Our birthday is on the Fourth of July.

6. I was born first.

7. Four minutes later, Carla was born.

8. We are fraternal twins.

9. No one thinks that we look very much alike.

10. Some identical twins dress alike.

11. We do not!

12. We each have our own personalities.

13. Being a twin is okay with me.

14. My sister is pretty cool.

15. We like to play basketball together.

16. Our mom calls us "Double Touble."

Name _____

Tune Up the Band

> The **complete subject** of a sentence tells what or who the sentence is about. The **complete predicate** tells what the subject is or does. Both may be one word or many.
> (complete subject)   (complete predicate)
> _Gifted musicians_ _create beautiful music._

In each of the following sentences, underline the complete subject once; underline the complete predicate twice.

The band students made a tremendous racket during their warm-up.

The drum major banged his baton on the ground.

Every drummer beat his drums loudly.

Clarinets squeaked and squawked.

Each one of the flute players practiced a scale.

Ten trombones blared.

Behind them, several tubas boomed.

A pair of cymbals clanged along.

Several saxophones sounded nearby.

Loudest of all, the trumpets blasted with all their might.

All that noise made everyone's ears hurt.

      83   IF87132 *Grammar*

Name _____

Snorkeling in Maui

> A **coordinating conjunction** is a word that joins words or groups of words together. They include: **and**, **but**, **or**, **nor**, **for**, **yet**, and **so**. These conjunctions connect words or sentences that are alike.
> *Snorkeling and scuba diving* are great ways to experience marine life firsthand.

Circle the coordinating conjunctions in each of the following sentences.

Brett and Kamal went snorkeling in the ocean. They wore masks and snorkels but no fins. Both of them hoped to see beautiful fish or colorful coral, so they swam toward the rocks. The sun overhead was hot, but the water was clear and cool. Diving into the ocean felt refreshing, but tasting the salty water did not. Brett swam after an interesting school of fish, so Kamal dove after him. The boys had to decide whether to continue diving or return to the boat. When they returned, they discussed the corals and tropical fish they had seen. Some snorkelers had seen big sea turtles, but Brett and Kamal had not. They hoped to use their underwater cameras and to snap pictures tomorrow. This was not their first snorkeling trip, nor would it be their last.

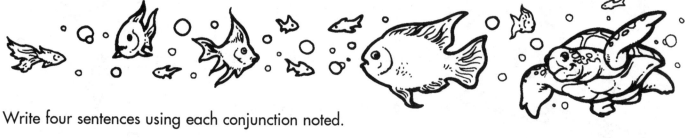

Write four sentences using each conjunction noted.

1. (and) _____

2. (but) _____

3. (or) _____

4. (so) _____

Name _____

Aesop's Fables

> A **compound subject** consists of two or more subjects joined by a conjunction. These subjects share a verb.
> ***Lessons and morals*** *are taught in Aesop's fables.*

In each of the following sentences, circle the conjunction and underline the two subjects it joins.

1. The town mouse and the country mouse like their own homes best.
2. The lion and the mouse demonstrate the importance of kindness.
3. The monkey and the dolphins show how one lie leads to another.
4. The bear and the bees learn to control their anger.
5. A hare and a tortoise race one another to the finish line.
6. Aesop's cat and old rat teach us that wise people don't fall for the same trick twice.
7. The mole and his mother tell us how foolish it is to boast.
8. The north wind and the sun prove that gentleness and kindness are more powerful than force.

Combine the two sentences by creating a compound subject in each. Use the conjunction noted at the beginning of each sentence. You may need to change the verb to a plural form.

(and) 1. The fifth grade class is studying Aesop's fables. The sixth grade class is studying Aesop's fables.

_____

(or) 2. Joe has the book. Frank has the book.

_____

(and) 3. The boys like the fables. The girls like the fables.

_____

(or) 4. David will read the fable aloud. Bradley will read the fable aloud.

_____

(and) 5. Mrs. Davis's class will act out some fables. Mr. Sim's class will act out some fables.

_____

(or) 6. Candace will be a frog. Sandra will be a frog.

_____

(and) 7. The moms will come to watch. The dads will come to watch.

_____

compound predicate

Name _____

A Day at the Beach

A **compound predicate** is two verbs joined by a conjunction and having the same subject.
I went to the beach <u>and</u> swam in the ocean.

Underline the compound predicate in each of the following sentences and circle the conjunction.

1. On our trip to the beach, we went snorkeling and tried surfing.

2. We saw many beautiful fish and enjoyed the warm ocean water.

3. All day, the sun shone brightly and warmed us.

4. Mom and I lay on the beach and got a tan.

5. Dad and my little brother looked for shells and built a sand castle.

6. For dinner, we sat outside and ate hamburgers by the ocean.

7. Some people watched the waves and waited for the sunset.

8. Finally, the sun turned red and seemed to sink into the ocean.

Write four sentences about the beach that contain compound predicates.

1. _____

2. _____

3. _____

4. _____

Name _____

The Tall Tulip Tale

A **simple sentence** contains one independent clause. A **compound sentence** contains two independent clauses that are closely related, but which usually have different subjects. A conjunction usually, but not always, joins the two clauses in a compound sentence. Remember to put a comma after the first clause and before the conjunction that joins the two clauses. If the subject of the two clauses is the same, but is restated (usually with a pronoun) the sentence is still joined by a comma and conjunction.

> *simple:* Uncle Sid loves to garden.
> *compound:* Uncle Sid loves to garden, and Auntie Sue loves to fill their house with flowers.

On the line before each sentence, write **S** if it is a simple sentence; write **C** if it is a compound sentence. Place a comma in the correct part of each compound sentence.

_____ 1. Uncle Sid always plants tulip bulbs around the house.

_____ 2. Auntie Sue loves the tulips and she looks forward to their blooming.

_____ 3. Uncle Sid put the bulbs in the ground in October.

_____ 4. All winter long, the sleeping tulips waited for the warm spring sun.

_____ 5. At last, they all began to push slowly through the earth but one tulip burst through in a big way.

_____ 6. Underneath the kitchen window, an enormous yellow tulip grew rapidly.

_____ 7. Soon the plant grew past the window and hovered above the house.

_____ 8. Auntie Sue gasped but fortunately she did not faint.

_____ 9. "Sid, come quick!" she shouted.

_____ 10. Uncle Sid stared up at the tulip and scratched his head.

_____ 11. Reporters arrived at the house and Uncle Sid's amazing yellow tulip was on the evening news.

_____ 12. Uncle Sid told everyone that the huge flower had been a gift for his Sue but that he didn't expect it to be quite so special.

_____ 13. Thanking him for her beautiful, tree-sized tulip, Auntie Sue gave Uncle Sid a big kiss.

Name _____

Deutschland

> When two simple sentences with different subjects are combined by a conjunction, they form a **compound sentence**. A comma is usually always placed before the conjunction.
>
> *Uncle Otto danced in his lederhosen.   I joined in, too.*
> *Uncle Otto danced in his lederhosen, and I joined in, too.*

Tell whether each sentence is simple or compound by writing **S** (simple) or **C** (compound) on the line.

_____1. My parents speak German, and I love to listen to them.

_____2. Grandpa tells folk tales and sings German songs.

_____3. Sauerbraten is delicious, and I like to eat it often.

_____4. Many great composers and musicians have come from Germany.

_____5. Education in Germany is controlled by the states, but every child must go to school for at least nine or ten years.

Use a comma and the conjunction in parentheses to combine each pair of sentences. Write the compound sentence on the line.

1. My grandma makes homemade sauerkraut. I prefer red cabbage. (but)

   _____

   _____

2. Do you plan to visit Germany? Would France appeal to you more? (or)

   _____

   _____

3. Berlin is Germany's capital. About three and a half million people live there. (and)

   _____

   _____

4. My family is from New York. Our ancestors lived in the Thuringer Forest. (but)

   _____

   _____

5. The Black Forest is a mountainous region. The North German Plain is low and nearly flat. (but)

   _____

   _____

Name _____

Club Members Only

> A **sentence** is a group of words containing a subject and a predicate and expressing a complete thought. A **fragment** is a group of words that does not express a complete thought. Fragments are missing either a subject or a verb.
>
> *My friends and I formed a special club. (sentence)*
> *Helping other people. (fragment)*

Write **S** before each group of words that is a sentence. Write **F** before each group of words that is a fragment.

_____ 1. Club members must use the secret password.

_____ 2. They greet other members with the secret handshake.

_____ 3. Every Saturday morning at the club treehouse.

_____ 4. Everyone shows kindness to all club members.

_____ 5. Club members bring fifty cents to every Saturday meeting for the Helping Fund.

_____ 6. When the Helping Fund gets really full.

_____ 7. We will spend the Fund money to help someone out.

_____ 8. Members vote on the best way to spend the money we have collected.

_____ 9. Sometimes we will do volunteer projects.

_____10. Raking leaves or pulling weeds for elderly people.

_____11. Other jobs too.

_____12. Our motto is "To help others above all."

_____13. Occasionally, we just hang out and have fun.

_____14. Skating in the school parking lot or eating at the clubhouse once in a while.

_____15. It is fun.

_____16. Being a club member.

Name _____

Mother Nature

A **run-on** is two or more complete sentences written without proper punctuation. Run-on sentences may be corrected by breaking the sentence, by utilizing a semicolon, or by adding a comma and a conjunction. The semicolon and the comma-conjunction pair should only be used when the ideas in the run-on are closely related. A comma should never be used without a conjunction to correct a run-on.

> **run-on:** *Reneé is skillfull, he likes to garden.*
> **correct:** *Reneé is skillful. He likes to garden.*
>
> **run-on:** *Joey is usually serious he is funny sometimes.*
> **correct:** *Joey is usually serious, but he is funny sometimes.*

Read the following sentences and determine if they are run-ons or not. If the sentence is a run-on, write **RO** in the blank before the sentence. If not, write **C** for correct.

_____ 1. Raking leaves is not easy, you must work for a long time in the cold outdoors.

_____ 2. I love to go fishing; it invigorates me.

_____ 3. He had just seen a skunk, it was coming down the street.

_____ 4. Maria plants flowers and raises vegetables in her garden.

_____ 5. Ramón loves books about birds he just read one about bald eagles.

_____ 6. Kyle likes to mountain climb, he is afraid of heights.

_____ 7. Patricia collects leaves, and she presses them in a book.

_____ 8. I want to go hiking, I also want to go bird watching.

Correct the run-on sentences on the lines below.

1. Janice stole my ant farm, she set all the ants free.

_____

_____

2. My mom loves petunias she likes to plant them in window boxes.

_____

_____

3. Our first garden was very large, planting all those vegetables was hard work.

_____

_____

4. Soon we will harvest our tomatoes, I just love fresh tomato sauce!

_____

_____

Name _____

It's in the Bag

There are four types of sentences.

Declarative —A declarative sentence makes a statement and ends with a period.

Interrogative —An interrogative sentence asks a question and ends with a question mark.

Imperative —An imperative sentence commands or requests. It ends with a period or an exclamation point. The subject *you* is always implied.

Exclamatory —An exclamatory sentence can either be a statement or a command made with strong feeling. It ends with an exclamation point.

declarative: There is a paper bag on the table.
interrogative: What is in that bag?
imperative: Take the bag off the table.
exclamatory: Be careful not to drop it!

Write the number of each sentence inside the correct bag to identify the sentence type.

1. What's in the bag?
2. It sounds like it is moving.
3. Look and see.
4. Whoa, be careful!
5. Do you think it's alive?
6. I don't dare look.
7. Just hurry up and open the bag!
8. Please hand me that stick.
9. Whenever I poke the bag, it makes a scratching noise.
10. Shhh!
11. Are you ever going to look inside that thing?
12. Wow, it's a rat!
13. It must be food for Ronald's snake.
14. I think that's gross!
15. Should I set him free?
16. Let me do it.

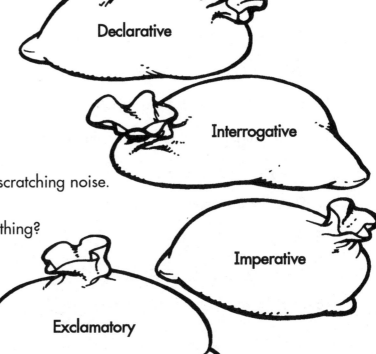

Name _____

It's a Bug's Life

> A **declarative sentence** makes a statement and ends with a period.
> *Catching bugs is fun.*

For each of the following sentences, add the proper punctuation. Write **yes** if it is a declarative sentence; write **no** if it is not.

_____ 1. Is that a stink bug

_____ 2. Some insects called bugs are not really bugs

_____ 3. Not all insects are bugs

_____ 4. Are bedbugs really bugs

_____ 5. Many birds eat bugs

_____ 6. Take that ugly bug outside please

_____ 7. Junebugs are not bugs

_____ 8. My sister really bugs me

_____ 9. Do you think ants are bugs

_____10. My stepsister Lucy gets totally freaked out by most bugs

_____11. What is the difference between an insect and a bug

_____12. Bugs are very useful little creatures, even if they are slightly pesky

_____13. Some bugs suck blood from animals and plants

_____14. Are you feeling itchy

_____15. Don't let the bedbugs bite

_____16. All bugs are insects

_____17. How many legs do bugs have

_____18. Bugs have two pairs of different wings

Name _____

Who Are You?

> An **interrogative sentence** asks a question and ends with a question mark.
>
> *What is an interrogative sentence?*

For each of the following sentences, write **yes** if it is interrogative or **no** if it is not. Add ending punctuation. Then, answer each question with a *declarative* sentence of your own.

_____ 1. State your full name

_____

_____ 2. When were you born

_____

_____ 3. In which city and state were you born

_____

_____ 4. Who are the other people in your family

_____

_____ 5. State the name of your first teacher

_____

_____ 6. What is your favorite subject at school

_____

_____ 7. List your hobbies

_____

_____ 8. With whom do you like to spend your time

_____

_____ 9. Describe your greatest talent

_____

_____10. What is the very best thing about you

_____

_____11. Whom would you most like to be like

_____

_____ 12. Explain what job you hope to have when you are an adult

_____

Name _____

Sudsing Up

> An **imperative sentence** commands or requests. It ends with a period or an exclamation point. The subject *you* is always implied.
> *Wash the car.*

In the following sentences, write **yes** if it is imperative; write **no** if it is not.

When You Wash A Car Remember:

____ 1. Don't forget to roll up the window.
____ 2. Use a soft sponge.
____ 3. Please avoid harsh detergents.
____ 4. Your car will look best if you wash the windows too.
____ 5. Water spots do not look good.
____ 6. Always dry the car off completely.

Change each one of the following questions into commands or requests. Be sure to use correct capitalization and the proper punctuation.

1. Could you please help me wash the car?

   _____

2. Will you bring the bucket here?

   _____

3. Do you mind filling it with soap and water?

   _____

4. Will you wash the tires with that brush please?

   _____

5. Will you wait until I finish sudsing up the car?

   _____

6. Would you please rinse the soap off with the sprayer?

   _____

7. Do you mind helping me dry off the car?

   _____

8. Will you accept $10.00 for helping me?

   _____

Name _____

A Close Call

An **exclamatory sentence** can be either a statement or a command made with strong feeling. It ends with an exclamation point.

Wait just one minute!
You've got to be kidding!
Look out!

Add ending punctuation to the following sentences. Then put a star next to each exclamatory sentence.

1. My dog, tony, is a poodle

2. He doesn't like to be touched

3. Oh no, he's mad now

4. Please don't pester the dog

5. Stop it right now

6. What if he bites you

7. Sit tony

8. Leave him alone

9. Ow

10. It's okay tony; settle down

11. Pass the dog treats please

12. Whoa, that was a close call

13. At least he didn't break the skin

95

Name _____

Rain, Rain, Don't Go Away!

A **comma** is used...
- • to set off an introductory phrase or independent clause.
  - • *After a hard rain, the earth smells fresh.*
- • after introductory words or phrases such as *yes, indeed, well, in addition, thus,* and *moreover.*
  - • *Yes, it is supposed to rain today.*
- • after words of direct address.
  - • *Melissa, come play in the rain with me.*
- • in a series—to separate words.
  - • *I have a raincoat, boots, and an umbrella.*

Add commas to the following sentences.

Yes I love a rainy day!

The rain taps on the windows plays on the sidewalk and dances on the roof.

I watch wait and wonder what the warm rain will bring.

Maxi why don't you hop up here and enjoy the rain with me.

My cat hopped onto the windowsill began purring and fell asleep.

No she didn't care about the falling raindrops at all.

For the next hour or so I snuggled into the window seat and listened to the rain's song.

Its song is sweet steady and strong.

"Sara come down for dinner," Mom called.

As I left my room I whispered to the rain,

"Rain please don't go away!"

Name _____

Maxwell T. Stewart

Use two **commas** to set off interrupting words or expressions and appositive phrases.

You can see, I'm sure, that rats spread disease.
The rat, a nocturnal animal, sleeps all day.

Add commas to the following sentences.

1. Maxwell the lazy rat slept all day in the alley behind Tony's Pizzeria.

2. He hid during the day under the steps by the back door.

3. No one including the other rats ever bothered him.

4. He Maxwell T. Stewart called himself King of the Rats.

5. This rat king a real scoundrel was bigger and fiercer than any other alley rat.

6. At night when the darkness came Maxwell prowled.

7. The nightlife especially the smells of the pizzeria brought him out.

8. He rummaged through the best eateries in town the local trash cans.

9. After a night of indulging Maxwell grew fat and sleepy.

10. Maxwell T. Stewart King of the Rats slinked past the other alley creatures and into his home beneath the steps of Tony's Pizzeria.

Name _____

Mom's Photo Album

When writing a **date**, use a **comma** to separate the day of the week from the month. A comma also separates the date from the year.

Wednesday, February 3, 1999
Tuesday, April 13, 1993

Capitalize and add commas to the dates below.

wednesday february 14 1968

tuesday september 4 1973

monday may 30 1977

thursday december 25 1980

wednesday august 28 1985

sunday november 27 1988

wednesday march 20 1991

saturday july 4 1992

thursday october 31 1996

sunday april 4 1999

saturday january 1 2000

tuesday february 13 2001

98

Name _____

Mailbag

> When writing an address, use a comma to separate the name of the city from the name of the state or country. Never put a comma between the state and the zip code.
>
> *Miss Spinella Spider*
> *8542 Thread Lane*
> *Web Corner, California 90210*

Write the addresses correctly on the envelopes to the right. Don't forget capitals and punctuation.

From: mr and mrs thomas cat
 1234 feline drive
 meowville texas 56543

To: marvin mouse sr
 873 rodent road
 squeaker town new york 38214

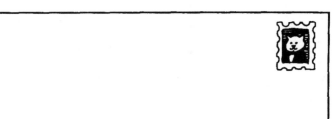

From: dr harold hedgehog
 7117 bristle boulevard
 prickly park wisconsin 87675

To: miss priscilla porcupine
 111 aquilla avenue
 smart city minnesota 75320

From: freddy falcon
 2020 laguna landings
 cliffside california 27022

To: wise old owl
 42 hoot lane
 treehole maine 40000

Name _____

We Wanna Know Your Name

Use a capital letter and a period for a title that is abbreviated. Use a capital and a period when an initial is used in place of a person's name. Always put a comma before a title if it appears after a person's name.

Roger T. Applegate, Jr.
Dr. Katherine R. Williams

Rewrite the following names and initials correctly inside the name tags.

mrs o sanford

HELLO MY NAME IS:
_____

dr philip prince

_____

bj taylor jr

_____

capt douglas walker

_____

marco garcia sr

_____

gov george r rice

VOTE FOR
_____

miss mz vandermeer

_____

rev james tiesdale

_____

carlos j lucas jr

_____

prof rr chapman

_____

maj michael b paris

_____

adm juliet n love

_____

IF87132 *Grammar*

Name _____

Borice's Book Bag

> Capitalize and underline or italicize the titles of books, magazines, and newspapers. The first word, the last word, and all other important words in a title are capitalized. Articles (the), conjunctions (and) and prepositions (of) are not capitalized unless they are the first or last word of the title.
>
> *Out of the Dust*
> *People*
> *The Chicago Tribune*

Rewrite the titles from Borice's book bag correctly on the corresponding lines below.

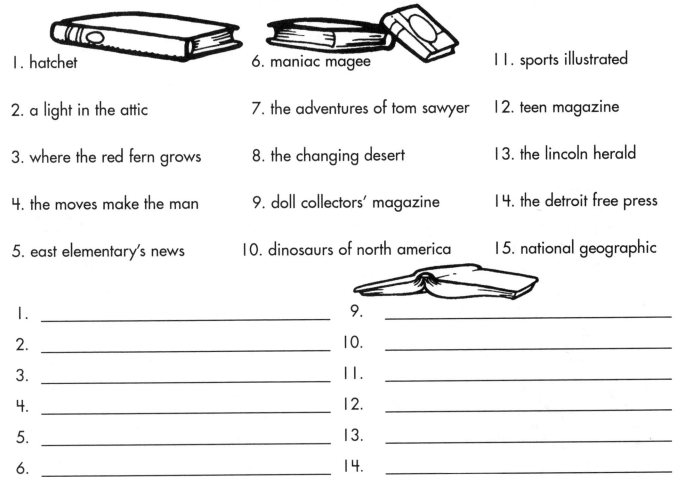

1. hatchet

2. a light in the attic

3. where the red fern grows

4. the moves make the man

5. east elementary's news

6. maniac magee

7. the adventures of tom sawyer

8. the changing desert

9. doll collectors' magazine

10. dinosaurs of north america

11. sports illustrated

12. teen magazine

13. the lincoln herald

14. the detroit free press

15. national geographic

1. _____
2. _____
3. _____
4. _____
5. _____
6. _____
7. _____
8. _____
9. _____
10. _____
11. _____
12. _____
13. _____
14. _____
15. _____

Name _____

The Long and Short of It

Abbreviations of proper nouns are capitalized. Abbreviations of common nouns are not. Special titles and degrees are also capitalized. Abbreviations should not be used in sentences.

Senator = Sen.   *centimeter = cm*

Write the abbreviations for the following words.

feet _____   November _____   Captain _____

Senior _____   Junior _____   September _____

Monday _____   Misses _____   court _____

street _____   avenue _____   January _____

Tuesday _____   Reverend _____   week _____

ounce _____   inch _____   Saturday _____

August _____   Wednesday _____   year _____

dozen _____   et cetera _____

Mister _____   February _____

December _____   Thursday _____

pound _____   yard _____

Friday _____   October _____

month _____   mile _____

Sunday _____   Doctor _____

IF87132 *Grammar*

Name _____

Chocolate Caramel Divine

> Quotation marks are used to enclose **direct quotation**. The end punctuation of the sentence usually comes before the final quotation mark at the end of the quote.
>
> Always capitalize the first word of direct quotation. Do not capitalize the first word in an interrupted quote, unless the second part begins a new sentence.
>
> *"It is time to go to the store!" Mom announced.*
> *"When we get there," she continued, "pick out your favorite ice cream."*
> *"We won't forget." replied Nate. "We love ice cream."*

Add the correct punctuation and capitalization to the following sentences. Write the corrected sentences on the lines.

1. would you help me choose some ice cream asked chloe

   _____

2. sure answered nate let's get something with caramel

   _____

3. caramel is good replied chloe but i prefer chocolate

   _____

4. how about something with both suggested nate

   _____

5. that's a great idea chloe responded

   _____

6. hey said nate i found one called chocolate caramel divine

   _____

7. that sounds perfect chloe agreed

   _____

8. where are you going now nate shouted

   _____

9. to get some hot fudge to pour on top chloe yelled back

   _____

10. don't forget a jar of caramel too nate called.

    _____

Answer Key

A Basketball Hero

There are eight main parts of speech:

noun	adjective	adverb
verb	preposition	interjection
pronoun	conjunction	

Name the part of speech for every word that is underlined. Record your answers on the lines below.

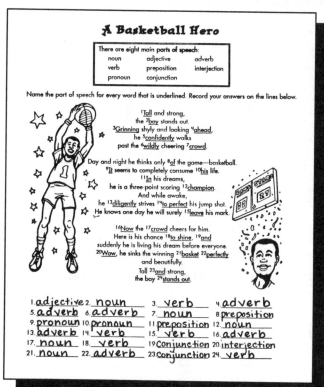

¹Tall and strong,
the ²boy stands out.
³Grinning shyly and looking ⁴ahead,
he ⁵confidently walks
past the ⁶wildly cheering ⁷crowd.

Day and night he thinks only ⁸of the game—basketball.
⁹It seems to completely consume ¹⁰his life.
¹¹In his dreams,
he is a three-point scoring ¹²champion.
And while awake,
he ¹³diligently strives ¹⁴to perfect his jump shot.
He knows one day he will surely ¹⁵leave his mark.

¹⁶Now the ¹⁷crowd cheers for him.
Here is his chance ¹⁸to shine, ¹⁹and
suddenly he is living his dream before everyone.
²⁰Wow, he sinks the winning ²¹basket ²²perfectly
and beautifully.
Tall ²³and strong,
the boy ²⁴stands out.

1. adjective 2. noun   3. verb   4. adverb
5. adverb   6. adverb   7. noun   8. preposition
9. pronoun   10. pronoun 11. preposition 12. noun
13. adverb   14. verb   15. verb   16. adverb
17. noun   18. verb   19. conjunction 20. interjection
21. noun   22. adverb   23. conjunction 24. verb

Page 4

Who, What, Where?

Nouns are words that name people, places, things, or ideas.
people: man, Tom, doctor
places: store, pharmacy, school
things and ideas: flashlight, trust, smile, pain

Write each noun under the correct category.

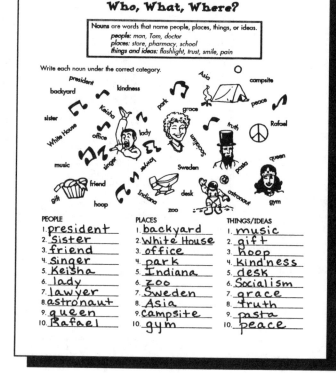

PEOPLE
1. president
2. sister
3. friend
4. singer
5. Keisha
6. lady
7. lawyer
8. astronaut
9. queen
10. Rafael

PLACES
1. backyard
2. White House
3. office
4. park
5. Indiana
6. zoo
7. Sweden
8. Asia
9. campsite
10. gym

THINGS/IDEAS
1. music
2. gift
3. hoop
4. kindness
5. desk
6. socialism
7. grace
8. truth
9. pasta
10. peace

Page 5

A Happy Arrival

Gender refers to the sex indicated by a noun. In English, there are four genders: *masculine* (male), *feminine* (female), *neuter* (no sex), and *indefinite* (either sex).

masculine: boy, man, brother
feminine: girl, woman, sister
neuter: pencil, comb, water
indefinite: person, painter, winner

Rewrite each noun from the Noun Box under the correct category of gender.

IT'S A BOY!
1. father
2. knight
3. emperor
4. bull
5. lad
6. uncle

IT'S A GIRL!
1. maiden
2. ewe
3. princess
4. niece
5. actress
6. mother

Noun Box

father	maiden	bull	cousin	nurse	cola
book	candle	ewe	singer	lad	mask
friend	champion	violin	princess	niece	actress
knight	emperor	seaweed	doctor	uncle	mother

IT'S AN IT!
1. book
2. candle
3. violin
4. seaweed
5. cola
6. mask

WHAT IS IT?
1. friend
2. champion
3. cousin
4. singer
5. doctor
6. nurse

Page 6

People, Places, and Things

Proper nouns are the names of specific people, places, or things. They are spelled with a capital letter. Your name is a proper noun. All other nouns are called **common nouns**. Common nouns do not name specific people, places, or things, and are not usually spelled with an initial capital letter.

proper nouns: New Hampshire, Michael Jordan, Central Park
common nouns: state, athlete, park

Write a proper noun for every common noun provided. Then, complete the remaining two noun pairs by providing your own common and proper nouns.

Answers will vary.

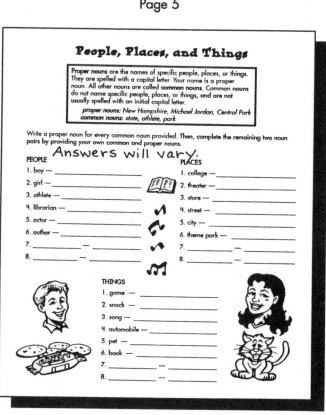

PEOPLE
1. boy —
2. girl —
3. athlete —
4. librarian —
5. actor —
6. author —
7.
8.

PLACES
1. college —
2. theater —
3. store —
4. street —
5. city —
6. theme park —
7.
8.

THINGS
1. game —
2. snack —
3. song —
4. automobile —
5. pet —
6. book —
7.
8.

Page 7

IF87132 *Grammar*

More Than One

Plural nouns are nouns indicating two or more people, places, things, or ideas.
1. To form the plural of most nouns, just add **s**.
2. Add **es** to a noun that ends in **s, x, ch, z, sh,** or **ss**.
3. If the noun ends in a **y** that is preceded by a vowel, change the **y** to an **i** and add **es**.
4. Add **es** to a noun that ends in an **o** preceded by a consonant.
5. Add **s** to a noun that ends in an **o** preceded by a vowel.

Change the singular nouns below into plural nouns.

radio	radios	family	families
sandwich	sandwiches	beard	beards
lady	ladies	mailbox	mailboxes
planet	planets	cargo	cargoes
kite	kites	city	cities
country	countries	jelly	jellies
pansy	pansies	umbrella	umbrellas
sound	sounds	glass	glasses
buzz	buzzes	dish	dishes
stereo	stereos	candy	candies
video	videos	dress	dresses
crash	crashes	hero	heroes
lunch	lunches	echo	echoes
light	lights	berry	berries
potato	potatoes	candy	candies

Page 8

A Red-Letter Day

Possessive nouns show ownership. They describe who or what possesses something. To form a possessive, add **'s** to the end of the noun. If a noun is plural and already ends in an **s**, simply add an apostrophe.
singular possessive: Valentine's Day is a great holiday.
plural possessive: I like to look at my classmates' valentines.

Place apostrophes where they belong in each possessive noun below.

It was Valentine's Day, and Miss Jackson's class was having a party. One of the party's events was a contest for wearing the most interesting red item. Miss Jackson was impressed with her students' participation. José's t-shirt was red, and Ling's socks were too. Tremel's hat, Maya's sweater, and Shaina's shoes were all red. Some students' shirts and jeans were covered with red hearts made from construction paper. But, one boy's Valentine outfit stood out above the rest. Grant's body was covered from head to toe in red. On his feet he wore little Susie's red dragon slippers. Over his clothes he sported his mother's fuzzy red bathrobe, and on his head he wore his grandma's curly, red wig. Everyone in the class agreed that Grant's creativity earned him the big heart-shaped box of chocolates.

Page 9

At the Library

Commas are used to set apart nouns of address and introductory words or phrases. A noun of address is what a person's name is called when she is being spoken to.
Meredith, bring me that book.
Words like **yes, no, as usual,** and **well** are called introductory words (or phrases).
No, I'm busy right now.

In each sentence below, add commas where necessary.

1. Mrs. Peterson, can I check out this book?
2. You would do better, Tim, with an easier book.
3. Yes, I like books about exciting places.
4. However, I also enjoy reading biographies about famous people.
5. Don't forget your library card, Maria!
6. Please, I need this book right now!
7. Well, you sure are in a hurry.
8. Reading, Dena, can be very exciting.
9. Shakespeare, Lucy, was a great playwright.
10. As usual, your library books are late, Charlie.
11. By the way, your dog chewed the corner of this book.
12. Well, Trevor, at least the dog didn't eat it.
13. Monica, you cannot check out that book.
14. Janelle, what kind of books do you like?
15. I prefer mysteries, Kwan.

Page 10

All Together

A collective noun names a group of people or things. It may be used as a singular or plural noun, depending on the implied meaning.
The family is discussing where to have the reunion. (singular)
The family are all giving their opinions. (plural)

Write S (singular) or P (plural) on the line to show how each collective noun is being used.

S 1. My group is going to Disney World.
P 2. The crew are all going to work in different places.
P 3. The litter of puppies are all running helter-skelter.
P 4. My family are all talking to each other.
S 5. The class is going on a trip.

Rewrite each sentence, using the correct verb or pronoun from the parentheses.

1. The faculty (is, are) required to turn in their grades by next week.
   The faculty are required to turn in their grades by next week.
2. A number of them (has, have) gone their separate ways.
   A number of them have gone their separate ways.
3. The team celebrates (its, their) victory.
   The team celebrates its victory.
4. A couple of students (owns, own) dogs.
   A couple of students own dogs.
5. The company (is, are) dispersing to their homes.
   The company are dispersing to their homes.
6. The boy scout troop (has, have) a bus of its own.
   The boy scout troop has a bus of its own.
7. The herd (was, were) returning to their individual stalls.
   The herd were returning to their individual stalls.
8. The crowd was on (its, their) feet.
   The crowd was on its feet.

Page 11

IF87132 *Grammar*

Illumination

A **direct object** is a noun or pronoun that follows a transitive verb. It tells *what* or *whom* receives the action of the verb. To find the direct object, ask *what* or *whom* after the action verb.

My mom turns on my light to wake me for school.
(turns on what?)
My mom wakes me for school by turning on my light.
(wakes whom?)

In each of the following sentences, underline all the verbs or verb phrases and draw a box around the direct object.

1. When we go camping, we take a lantern.
2. Mom lights candles when the power goes out.
3. I have a nightlight in my bedroom.
4. The flashlight needs two batteries to work.
5. Bright spotlights illuminated the stage during the play.
6. The sun lights and warms our world.
7. Our Christmas bulbs create a lovely glow.
8. Twinkling stars filled the clear evening sky.
9. Several rows of candles on the cake lit the room.
10. Sometimes a full moon illuminates the night all by itself.
11. We save energy at our house by turning off the lights when we leave a room.
12. Turn off the lights when you're done.
13. The parents calmed their children in the dark
14. In the cave, the small lamp leads the explorers through the blackness.
15. A bright, full moon amazed the stargazers.

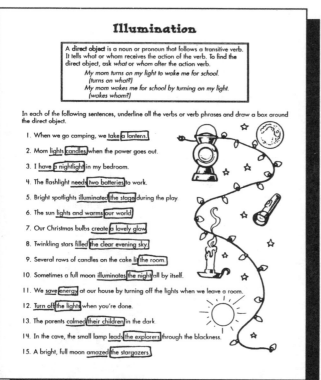

Page 12

Our Holiday

An **indirect object** is a noun or pronoun that names the person or object *to whom* or *for whom* (or *what*) something is done. To find the indirect object, ask *to* or *for whom* or *to* or *for what* after the action verb.

Allison bought Timmy a gift.
(bought for whom? Timmy)
I gave the charity some money.
(gave some money to what? the charity)

In each of the following sentences, circle the action verb and underline the indirect object.

1. In the morning, Dad read us a story.
2. Then, Mom served everyone cinnamon rolls and hot cocoa.
3. I gave the cat its favorite food.
4. Then, we gave each other our gifts.
5. Johnny found Mom a big box to open right away.
6. I made my sister a painted sweatshirt.
7. She gave me a diary.
8. Dad made mom a rocking chair.
9. She knit him a sweater.
10. My sister and brother and I wrote our parents a song.
11. We sang them it too.
12. Later, Mom cooked the family a delicious dinner.
13. After dinner, we gave Grandma a call.
14. Grandma had sent us presents.
15. Tomorrow we will write everyone who sent gifts thank-you notes.

Page 13

Looking Good!

A **direct object** is a noun or pronoun that follows an action verb. It tells *what* or *whom* receives the action of the verb. An **indirect object** is a noun or pronoun that names the person or thing *to whom* or *for whom* something is done.

I.O.   D.O.
I gave Louise a make-over yesterday.

In each of the following sentences, underline the direct object once and the indirect object twice. Circle all verbs. (Note: Some sentences do not have an indirect object.)

Louise needed a new look in the worst way.
She asked me to help.
I gave her my suggestions.
First we brushed her hair.
Her wild hair gave the brush a real workout.
Then we pulled her hair back with a tie-dyed ribbon.
"Wash your face too," I suggested.

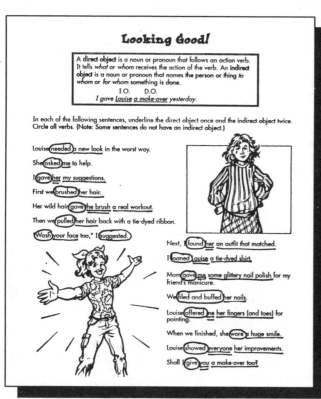

Next, I found her an outfit that matched.
I loaned Louise a tie-dyed shirt.
Mom gave me some glittery nail polish for my friend's manicure.
We filed and buffed her nails.
Louise offered me her fingers (and toes) for painting.
When we finished, she wore a huge smile.
Louise showed everyone her improvements.
Shall I give you a make-over too?

Page 14

On-the-Road Adventure

A **noun** is a word that names a person, place, thing, or idea. A **verb** is a word that states an action or a state of being. Some words can act as either nouns or verbs.

noun: a bark, a ride, a snack, love
verb: to bark, to ride, to snack, to love

In the story below, mark the underlined words N (noun) or V (verb) to indicate how each word is used in the sentence.

I had to dress [V] by 10:00 a.m. I passed by my yellow dress [N] and slipped on a pair [N] of jeans. I paired [V] them with a tank top. I had to hurry. At 10:30, Dad and I were leaving to canoe [V] and camp at the lake. We had purchased a special canoe [N] from the sporting goods store.

We were on the road for several hours, and I was just beginning to tire [V], when one of our tires [N] burst. I could hear the air stream [V] out of the tire as Dad moved the car to the side of the road by a stream [N].

We were miles from anywhere, so we decided to camp [V] right there. Dad set up a camp [N] just off the road in a small clearing with a few trees. I helped him push [V] the car off the road. He put the car in neutral, and I gave it a big push [N] onto the shoulder.

At the camp, we roasted marshmallows and started singing [V] campfire songs. Dad proclaimed my singing [N] better than his.

Write each noun/verb on the lines below. Add four words that can be either a noun or a verb.

dress   Stream   Answers
pair   camp   will
canoe   push   vary.
tire   singing

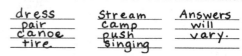

Page 15

On Your Toes!

A **verb** is a word that expresses an action or a state of being.
action: hug, baked, sings
being: is, was, seems

In each of the following sentences, circle the verb and indicate if it is an action (A) or a state of being (B) verb.

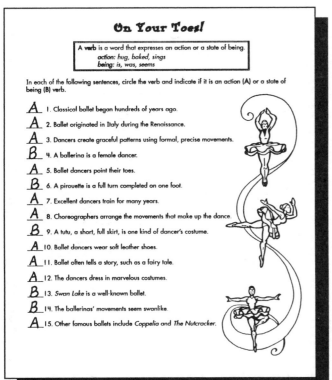

A 1. Classical ballet began hundreds of years ago.

A 2. Ballet originated in Italy during the Renaissance.

A 3. Dancers create graceful patterns using formal, precise movements.

B 4. A ballerina is a female dancer.

A 5. Ballet dancers point their toes.

B 6. A pirouette is a full turn completed on one foot.

A 7. Excellent dancers train for many years.

A 8. Choreographers arrange the movements that make up the dance.

B 9. A tutu, a short, full skirt, is one kind of dancer's costume.

A 10. Ballet dancers wear soft leather shoes.

A 11. Ballet often tells a story, such as a fairy tale.

A 12. The dancers dress in marvelous costumes.

B 13. *Swan Lake* is a well-known ballet.

B 14. The ballerinas' movements seem swanlike.

A 15. Other famous ballets include *Coppelia* and *The Nutcracker*.

Page 16

Make a Blue-Jean Bag

A **verb** is a word that expresses an action or a state of being. Some verbs are preceded by a helping verb.
action: sink, fought, cries
being: is, are, seemed
helping + verb: will run, can be, have written

In each of the following sentences, circle the verb. Draw a line from each sentence to the correct bag.

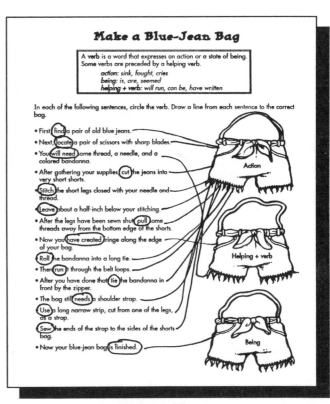

- First, (find) a pair of old blue jeans.
- Next, (locate) a pair of scissors with sharp blades.
- You (will need) some thread, a needle, and a colored bandanna.
- After gathering your supplies, (cut) the jeans into very short shorts.
- (Stitch) the short legs closed with your needle and thread.
- (Leave) about a half-inch below your stitching.
- After the legs have been sewn shut, (pull) some threads away from the bottom edge of the shorts.
- Now you (have created) fringe along the edge of your bag.
- (Roll) the bandanna into a long tie.
- Then (run) it through the belt loops.
- After you have done that, (tie) the bandanna in front by the zipper.
- The bag still (needs) a shoulder strap.
- (Use) a long narrow strip, cut from one of the legs, as a strap.
- (Sew) the ends of the strap to the sides of the shorts bag.
- Now your blue-jean bag (is finished).

Page 17

Verb Tents

The **tense** of a verb indicates the time an action takes place.
Present tense indicates action or being that is happening now. **Past tense** indicates action or being that was completed in the past. The **future tense** indicates action or being that will take place in the future.
present tense: Stacey camps outside.
past tense: Stacey camped outside.
future tense: Stacey will camp outside.

Fill in the verb tents with the missing verb forms, assuming *he* or *she* is the subject.

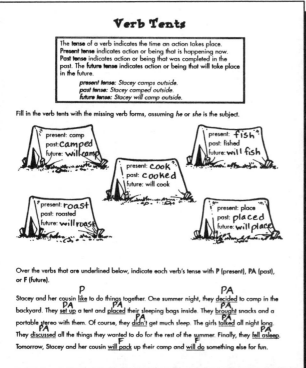

present: camp
past: camped
future: will camp

present: fish
past: fished
future: will fish

present: cook
past: cooked
future: will cook

present: roast
past: roasted
future: will roast

present: place
past: placed
future: will place

Over the verbs that are underlined below, indicate each verb's tense with P (present), PA (past), or F (future).

Stacey and her cousin <u>like</u>(P) to do things together. One summer night, they <u>decided</u>(PA) to camp in the backyard. They <u>set up</u>(PA) a tent and <u>placed</u>(PA) their sleeping bags inside. They <u>brought</u>(PA) snacks and a portable stereo with them. Of course, they <u>didn't get</u>(PA) much sleep. The girls <u>talked</u>(PA) all night long. They <u>discussed</u>(PA) all the things they wanted to do for the rest of the summer. Finally, they <u>fell</u>(PA) asleep. Tomorrow, Stacey and her cousin <u>will pack</u>(F) up their camp and <u>will do</u>(F) something else for fun.

Page 18

A Fine Hatch

The **tense** of a verb indicates the time the action of the sentence takes place. **Present tense** indicates action or being that is happening now. **Past tense** indicates action or being that was completed in the past. **Future tense** indicates action or being that will take place in the future. The auxiliary verb *will* is usually used with the principle verb to form the future tense.
present: Joseph plants corn.
past: Joseph planted corn.
future: Joseph will plant corn.

Identify the tense of the verb in each sentence: P (present), PA (past), or F (future).

PA 1. The mother robin laid her eggs in a nest on our front porch.

P 2. Unfortunately, whenever we go through the front door, she leaves her nest.

PA 3. Yesterday we noticed that there were five blue eggs in the nest.

PA 4. We have been concerned about the eggs staying warm enough.

F 5. The eggs will hatch in about two weeks.

PA 6. We did not remove the nest from the porch after she hatched her eggs last spring.

F 7. I will leave this nest alone since she may return again next spring.

PA 8. Last spring, four baby birds hatched.

P 9. I can't wait to see how many we will have this year.

P 10. For now, we are trying to stay away from the porch so the mother bird will stay on her nest and keep those eggs safe.

F 11. We will be careful not to touch the birds or the nest.

P 12. It is exciting to watch the babies grow.

P 13. It won't be long before the new birds will fly away.

Page 19

IF87132 *Grammar*

May I Sit, Set, Lie, or Lay?

Lie means to rest or recline while **lay** means to put or place.

Sit means to rest in a seated position while **set** means to place or put something.

May is used to ask permission while **can** refers to something you have the physical ability to do.

> I will **lie** down to rest as soon as I **lay** out some clean clothes for tomorrow.
> Please **sit** down while I **set** the table for dinner.
> Mom says we **may** put up the tent if we **can** figure out how to do it.

In the following sets of sentences, circle the correct verb.

1. Nancy (lay, **laid**) a table cloth on the ground and began to unpack the picnic basket.
2. The children's dog (lays, **lies**) on the grass nearby.
3. Little Kenneth (lays, **lies**) beside him looking at the fluffy clouds overhead.
4. Troy helped to (**lay**, lie) the sandwiches on plates.
5. Meanwhile, Rex, the dog, (lays, **lies**) under the big maple tree.
6. His favorite ball (**lays**, lies) next to him.

1. It's time to (set, **sit**) down for lunch.
2. Please (**set**, sit) the pepper and salt on the table.
3. The baby will (set, **sit**) in his high chair.
4. The girls want to (set, **sit**) next to each other.
5. Mom (**sets**, sits) the food in the middle of the table.
6. She is usually the last one to (set, **sit**) down.

1. After the picnic, we (can, **may**) take a walk on the trails.
2. (**Can**, May) you carry the water bottle?
3. Mom said we (can, **may**) take the binoculars too.
4. (Can, **May**) I have the camera?
5. I (**can**, may) take pretty good pictures.
6. If we hurry, we (**can**, may) see some interesting wildlife before it gets dark.

Page 20

O Canada!

The subject and verb of any clause must agree in number. If a subject is singular, the verb must be singular. If a subject is plural, the verb must be plural.

> The singer (singular) performs (singular) "O Canada."
> The singers (plural) perform (plural) "O Canada."

In the following sentences, decide if the subjects and verbs agree. If they agree, write YES. If they do not, write NO. Correct the sentences where the subject and verb do not agree.

NO 1. More than 28 million people lives in Canada.
YES 2. The government recognizes two official languages.
NO 3. Some Canadians speaks French.
YES 4. Others speak English.
NO 5. Canada are *is* divided into provinces and territories.
NO 6. The Native Americans makes up approximately two percent of the population.
YES 7. Many of Canada's schools are run by religious organizations.
YES 8. Many Canadians enjoy winter activities such as skiing and snowshoeing.
YES 9. Today, hockey is probably the most popular sport in Canada.
YES 10. The food of the Canadians is similar to that eaten by Americans.
YES 11. Many famous actors, authors, and musicians come from Canada.
NO 12. Canada have *has* six standard time zones.
NO 13. Just like the United States, there is *are* Rocky Mountains in Canada.
YES 14. Much of Canada maintains temperatures below 50° F (10° C) year round.
NO 15. Canada are *is* surrounded by water on three sides.
YES 16. Toronto, Canada is a popular vacation spot for many tourists.

Page 21

Just Your Average Day

A **regular verb** is one which forms its past and past participle tenses by adding ed or d to the present tense verb form.
> jump, jumped, (have, has, had) jumped
> watch, watched, (have, has, had) watched

Write the past and past participle forms of the following verbs.

PRESENT	PAST		PAST PARTICIPLE
1. wait	waited	(have, has, had)	waited
2. roam	roamed	(have, has, had)	roamed
3. create	created	(have, has, had)	created
4. believe	believed	(have, has, had)	believed
5. hunt	hunted	(have, has, had)	hunted
6. travel	traveled	(have, has, had)	traveled

Answers will vary.

Supply your own regular verbs to complete these sentences.

1. The children have _____ to school.
2. They have _____ hard all day.
3. During recess they _____ a game of tag.
4. For lunch they had _____ pizza.
5. In the afternoon, the class _____ the history of Rome.
6. Now the students have _____ home again.

Write one sentence for each verb given.

(skate) _____

(has obeyed) _____

(dance) _____

Page 22

Aberant Actions

An **irregular verb** is any verb which does not form its past and past participle tenses by adding d or ed to its present tense.
> wear, wore, (have, has, had) worn
> eat, ate, (have, has, had) eaten

Complete the chart.

PRESENT	PAST	PAST PARTICIPLE (have, has, had)
begin	began	begun
blow	blew	blown
do	did	done
draw	drew	drawn
drive	drove	driven
fly	flew	flown
forbid	forbade	forbidden
give	gave	given
go	went	gone
hide	hid	hidden
know	knew	known
lie	lay	lain
ride	rode	ridden
say	said	said
shake	shook	shaken
sing	sang	sung
speak	spoke	spoken
take	took	taken
tear	tore	torn

Page 23

Swimming Lessons

An **irregular verb** is any verb which does not form both its past and past participle tenses by adding *d* or *ed* to its present tense.
shake, shook, (have, has, had) shaken
fight, fought, (have, has, had) fought

Write the past and past participle form of each of the following verbs.

PRESENT	PAST		PAST PARTICIPLE
drink	drank	(have, has, had)	drunk
creep	crept	(have, has, had)	crept
freeze	froze	(have, has, had)	frozen
hide	hid	(have, has, had)	hidden
steal	stole	(have, has, had)	stolen
throw	threw	(have, has, had)	thrown
weave	wove	(have, has, had)	woven
write	wrote	(have, has, had)	written

Circle the correct verb in each sentence.

1. Many kids have (swimmed, *swum*) at the high school pool.
2. Mr. Steel has (*taught*, teached) swimming lessons for years.
3. No one has (wore, *worn*) bathing caps in any of my classes.
4. We had (*dived*, doven) into the deep end often.
5. I (feeled, *felt*) embarrassed when I did a belly flop.
6. We practiced rescuing a person who had (fell, *fallen*) into the water.
7. Fortunately, no one had (*sunk*, sunken) to the bottom for real.
8. My relay team had (*won*, winned) the backstroke race.
9. I (*drank*, drunk) a lot of pool water.
10. Sara was (*thrown*, throwed) into the deep end.

Page 24

Pete

A **contraction** is formed by joining two words. Some contractions are formed by adding the word *not* to a verb. An apostrophe takes the place of the *o* in *not*, which is dropped.
do + not = don't

Write the contraction of the underlined words on the line after each sentence.
1. To meet Pete is *not* a treat. **isn't**
2. Pete *does not* eat meat. **doesn't**
3. Pete *can not* eat wheat. **can't**
4. Pete *would not* even eat a beet. **wouldn't**
5. But, *do not* try to stop Pete from eating sweets. **don't**

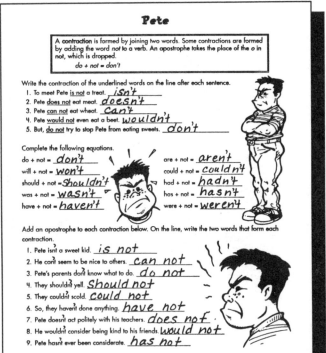

Complete the following equations.

do + not = **don't**		are + not = **aren't**
will + not = **won't**		could + not = **couldn't**
should + not = **shouldn't**		had + not = **hadn't**
was + not = **wasn't**		has + not = **hasn't**
have + not = **haven't**		were + not = **weren't**

Add an apostrophe to each contraction below. On the line, write the two words that form each contraction.
1. Pete isn't a sweet kid. **is not**
2. He can't seem to be nice to others. **can not**
3. Pete's parents don't know what to do. **do not**
4. They shouldn't yell. **should not**
5. They couldn't scold. **could not**
6. So, they haven't done anything. **have not**
7. Pete doesn't act politely with his teachers. **does not**
8. He wouldn't consider being kind to his friends. **would not**
9. Pete hasn't ever been considerate. **has not**

Page 25

The Night Sky

A **linking verb** does not show action. It connects a word or words in the predicate to the subject of the sentence. Some very common linking verbs are forms of *to be*: am, are, is, was, and were. If a verb can be replaced by a form of *to be*, it is usually a linking verb.
The night sky is a very beautiful sight.

In the following sentences, circle the linking verbs and underline the words that each links.

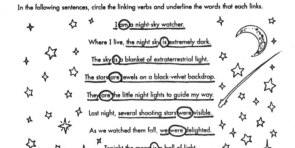

I *am* a night-sky watcher.

Where I live, the night sky *is* extremely dark.

The sky *is* a blanket of extraterrestrial light.

The stars *are* jewels on a black-velvet backdrop.

They *are* the little night lights to guide my way.

Last night, several shooting stars *were* visible.

As we watched them fall, we *were* delighted.

Tonight the moon *is* a ball of light.

Sometimes it *is* a sliver of brightness.

Not all linking verbs are forms of *to be*. Write **Yes** or **No** next to each sentence below to show if it contains a linking verb.
Yes 1. The dark night felt chilly.
No 2. The girl felt her way through the pitch-black tunnel.
Yes 3. The children grew sleepy.
No 4. We grow lilacs in our yard.
No 5. Suzie smelled the morning glories.
Yes 6. The breeze off the lake smelled wonderful.

Page 26

A Few Famous People

A **linking verb** does not show action; it connects a word or words in the predicate to the subject of the sentence. Some common linking verbs are forms of *to be*: am, are, is, was, and were.
A **predicate noun** is a noun following a linking verb. It tells something about the subject and may also be called a subject complement.
L.V. P.N.
Learning about famous people is a fun hobby.

In each of the following sentences, circle the linking verb and underline the predicate noun.
1. Michael Jordan *is* an amazing basketball player.
2. Steven Spielberg *is* an award-winning movie director.
3. Harriet Tubman *was* a brave woman who freed many slaves.
4. The Beatles *were* popular musicians from England.
5. One of the most loved presidents of the United States *is* Abraham Lincoln.
6. One impressive female athlete *is* the ice-skating Michelle Kwan.
7. Charles Lindbergh *was* the first person to fly non-stop across the Atlantic Ocean by himself.
8. A favorite author of many young people *is* Gary Paulsen.
9. The *Mona Lisa* *is* a well-known painting by Leonardo daVinci.
10. One former first lady of the United States of America *is* Nancy Reagan.
11. Snoopy *is* the most lovable beagle ever.
12. Theodore Roosevelt refused to shoot a chained bear; this *is* the origin of the term "teddy bear."

Write four original sentences containing the linking verb noted and a predicate noun.
(is) 1. *Answers will vary.*
(are) 2.
(was) 3.
(were) 4.

Page 27

IF87132 *Grammar*

Page 28

Tennis Anyone?

> A **linking verb** does not show action. It connects a word or words in the predicate to the subject of the sentence. Some very common linking verbs are forms of *to be*: **am, are, is, was,** and **were.**
> A **predicate adjective** follows a linking verb and describes the subject. It is also known as a subject complement.
> L.V. P.A.
> *Successful tennis players are disciplined.*

In each of the following sentences, circle the linking verb and underline the predicate adjective.

1. Their game of tennis (was) challenging.

2. The final game (was) exciting for the spectators.

3. Both of the players (were) competitive.

4. The sun (was) hot above the bleachers.

5. The loudly cheering crowd (was) huge.

6. Everyone (was) eager to see the winner claim his prize.

7. Each volley (was) strong.

8. Finally, one player (was) thrilled because he won the match.

9. The cash prize (was) sizable.

10. A win like that (is) wonderful for any tennis player.

Write five original sentences that contain the linking verb noted and a predicate adjective.

(am) 1. *Answers will vary.*

(is) 2. _____

(are) 3. _____

(was) 4. _____

(were) 5. _____

Page 29

The Bear Facts

> A **predicate noun** or **adjective** follows a linking verb and renames the subject.
> *predicate noun:* Mike is a bear hunter.
> *predicate adjective:* Mike is brave.

In each of the following sentences, circle the linking verb and underline either the predicate noun or the predicate adjective, whichever is used. On the line, write PN for each predicate noun and PA for each predicate adjective.

PN 1. Bears (are) mammals.

PN 2. They (are) large and powerful animals.

PN 3. A bear's home (is) a den.

PN 4. A den (is) a cave.

PA 5. Fully grown bears (are) strong.

PA 6. A bear's paw (is) powerful.

PA 7. Hungry bears (are) dangerous.

PA 8. All bears (are) short-tempered.

PA 9. Still, most bears (are) quite peaceful.

PN 10. Baby bears (are) cubs.

PA 11. When they are born, cubs (are) surprisingly small.

PA 12. A mother bear (is) protective of her cubs.

PA 13. Bear cubs (are) playful.

PN 14. Insects and grubs (are) delicious cub foods.

PN 15. Honey (is) a sweet bear treat.

PN 16. Bears (are) excellent fishers.

PN 17. They (are) good swimmers too.

PA 18. A bear's sense of smell (is) excellent.

Page 30

Amazing Animal Facts

> A **transitive verb** is an action verb that directs action toward a direct object.
> Mr. McGrady's dog chewed the shoes.

In each of the following sentences, underline the transitive verb and circle the direct object.

1. A gila monster stores (fat) in its tail.

2. The sticky feet of green tree frogs grip (smooth, slippery surfaces.)

3. A chimpanzee uses (sticks) to catch bugs.

4. Baby prairie dogs play (hide-and-seek.)

5. Elephants bury (their dead) with leaves and dirt.

6. The narwhal may use (its tusk) for fighting.

7. The addax, a desert antelope, never drinks (water.)

8. The Etruscan shrew eats (three times its own) weight each day.

9. Vampire bats drink (about a tablespoon of blood) a day.

10. An Alsation dog has (forty-four times more smell cells) than a human being.

11. The blue whale has (eyes as big as footballs.)

12. The ground squirrel in the Kalahari Desert uses (its tail) to shade it from the sun.

13. The tenrec, an insect-eater from Madagascar, uses (spit) rubbed into the bark of trees to mark its territory.

14. Prairie dogs exchange (a "kiss") when they meet in order to find out if they know each other.

15. The sea otter uses (a large stone) balanced on its stomach to smash open shellfish.

16. A male platypus has (poisonous spurs) on its back legs.

17. In 1875, a beagle from Switzerland climbed (Mont Blanc,) the highest mountain in the Alps.

18. A beaver once built (a dam) that was 2,296 feet (700 m) long.

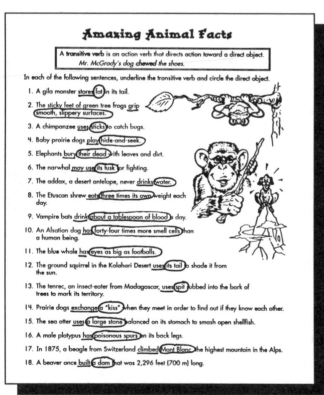

Page 31

Aunt Sally and Sam

> An **intransitive verb** is an action verb that does not have a direct object and does not direct action toward someone or something.
> *Parrots talk constantly.*
> *(Parrots talk can stand alone.)*

In the following sentences, underline each intransitive verb and circle each subject.

My (Aunt Sally) lives up the hill with her five dogs, twelve cats, and talking parrot Sam.

(Aunt Sally) paints in the early morning and in the late afternoon.

(She) works in her garden in between.

While she plants, (Sam) squawks out the window at her.

(He) screeches until she comes in the house.

In her kind way, (she) smiles at Sam.

Together (they) relax with the cats and dogs near the big picture window in the sitting room.

(They) watch as the sun sets.

(Sally) hums to her animal friends.

(Sam) sings along with her.

Another (day) ends peacefully on Aunt Sally's hill.

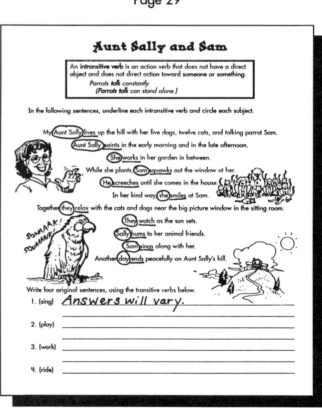

Write four original sentences, using the transitive verbs below.

1. (sing) *Answers will vary.*

2. (play) _____

3. (work) _____

4. (ride) _____

IF87132 *Grammar*

It's Easy Being Green

A **transitive verb** is followed by a direct object. An **intransitive verb** does not direct action toward an object.
transitive: I painted my bedroom green.
intransitive: My sister helped.

Determine if the following sentences are transitive (T) or intransitive (I). Write your response on the blank before each sentence.

T 1. I love to eat big garlic dill pickles on a hot summer day.
I 2. Most bullfrogs have bumpy, dark green skin.
T 3. Popeye eats spinach to stay tough and strong.
T 4. Sour limes make a tasty key-lime pie!
I 5. At our house, green jelly beans always get eaten first.
T 6. On St. Patrick's Day, many people celebrate the color green.
T 7. I like to have green dollar bills in my wallet.
I 8. Valuable emeralds are found in beautiful pieces of jewelry.
I 9. The cool green grass feels great on my toes.
I 10. The pond is decorated with luscious lilypads.
I 11. A grasshopper hides in the tall grasses.
T 12. Iggie, the pale green iguana, eats flies.
T 13. Green lights give permission to go.
I 14. A moldy fuzz grows in the refrigerator.
T 15. The color green symbolizes envy.
T 16. Sam I Am likes green eggs and ham.
I 17. Broccoli is good for you.
T 18. Making green slime is fun.

Page 32

Happily Ever After

A **participle** is a verb form that can act as an adjective. A **present participle** is the *ing* form of a verb. The past participle of most verbs ends in *d* or *ed*, and occasionally *t*, *en*, or *n*.
present: Fairy tales with enchanted castles and dancing maidens are my favorite.
past: My sister loves the tale of the slain giant.

Underline the participle in each of the following sentences and identify if each one is a present (PR) or past (PA) participle.

PR 1. A kiss awakened the sleeping princess, who had been in the tower for a hundred years.
PA 2. The witch offered Snow White a poisoned apple because she was jealous of the girl's beauty.
PA 3. The three bears surveyed the broken chair and the bowls of porridge.
PR 4. Under the moonlight, the dancing couple fell hopelessly in love.
PR 5. The people mock the self-exalting emperor and his royal new clothes.
PA 6. Because of her love for her father, Beauty went to live in the enchanted castle.
PR 7. Rapunzel lets down her flowing hair when the witch calls to her.
PR 8. In exchange for the maiden's first-born child, Rumpelstiltskin changed the straw into gold on his spinning wheel.
PA 9. Hansel and Gretel heard the evil witch's voice from within the candied cottage.
PR 10. The ugly ogre is fooled by a talking cat in boots and a hat.
PR 11. The princess's sleep is disturbed by an annoying pea under her mattresses.
PR 12. Thumbelina emerged from the beautiful opening blossom.

Write a short sentence for each participle noted below.
1. (baked) Answers will vary.
2. (chirping) _____
3. (singing) _____
4. (chosen) _____

Page 33

The Hundred Acre Wood

A **verb phrase** is a group of words that does the work of a single verb. The phrase includes one principal verb and one or more helping verbs.
*Stories of Winnie-the-Pooh **are set** in the Hundred Acre Wood.*

In each of the following sentences, underline the verb phrase and circle the helping verbs.

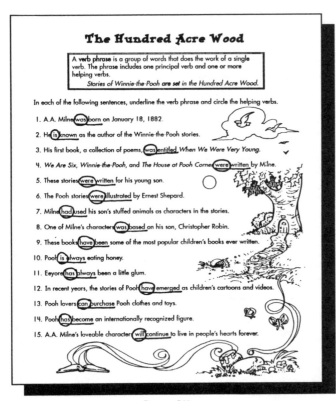

1. A.A. Milne (was) born on January 18, 1882.
2. He (is) known as the author of the Winnie-the-Pooh stories.
3. His first book, a collection of poems, (was) entitled When We Were Very Young.
4. We Are Six, Winnie-the-Pooh, and The House at Pooh Corner (were) written by Milne.
5. These stories (were) written for his young son.
6. The Pooh stories (were) illustrated by Ernest Shepard.
7. Milne (had) used his son's stuffed animals as characters in the stories.
8. One of Milne's characters (was) based on his son, Christopher Robin.
9. These books (have) (been) some of the most popular children's books ever written.
10. Pooh (is) (always) eating honey.
11. Eeyore (has) always been a little glum.
12. In recent years, the stories of Pooh (have) emerged as children's cartoons and videos.
13. Pooh lovers (can) purchase Pooh clothes and toys.
14. Pooh (has) become an internationally recognized figure.
15. A.A. Milne's loveable characters (will) continue to live in people's hearts forever.

Page 34

Mall Time

An **infinitive** is a present tense verb and is generally preceded by the word *to*. It may act as a noun, verb, adjective, or adverb.
To go to the mall is great.
I ordered Chinese to go at the Food Court.
She was happy to go with us.
I want to go to the stores.

Draw a box around the infinitives in each of the following sentences.

1. It's a blast to go shopping at the mall with my best friends.
2. Since we don't drive, our moms are glad to drop us off.
3. We agree on a few stores to check out right away.
4. Leza tries to find the perfect shoes.
5. Beth wants to buy a good book, but Kendra wants to save her money for some earrings.
6. I am determined to purchase a cool hat for my older brother's birthday present.
7. After awhile, our stomachs start to growl and we have to get something to eat.
8. My friends and I like to eat at the food court.
9. Of course, it's easy to enjoy a yummy lunch with all of the junk food there.
10. We usually try to share our food so that everyone gets to taste a little bit of everything.
11. Before we get ready to leave, we make one last stop at the chocolate shop.
12. Everybody spends a little money to buy the moms some chocolate truffles.
13. We want to show them how much we appreciate their driving us here.
14. I can't wait to come back to the mall again soon.

Page 35

IF87132 *Grammar*

Soaring Above the Clouds

Forms of the verb *be* can be used as linking or helping verbs.
Linking verbs link the subject to the predicate. Helping verbs are
added to the front of a verb to "help" it complete an action.
linking: Studying airplanes is Joel's favorite hobby.
helping: He is going to the county airshow.

Write **correct** or **incorrect** on the line to tell whether the form of *be* is used correctly in each
sentence.

1. You be tired after a long plane flight. **incorrect**
2. The flight is going to take off late. **correct**
3. She been waiting for the plane to land. **incorrect**
4. The plane has been cleaned and stocked with food. **correct**
5. We are going to fly to Hawaii. **correct**
6. Be you frightened of flying? **incorrect**
7. They are boarding the plane. **correct**
8. The pilot is turning on the no-smoking sign. **correct**

Write **linking** or **helping** on the line to tell how the form of *be* is used in each sentence.

1. Joel is flying over Lake Michigan. **helping**
2. The weather is good. **linking**
3. Aviation is Joel's favorite subject. **linking**
4. The plane was climbing in the air. **helping**
5. All the passengers' lap belts were fastened. **helping**
6. I am hoping to take flying lessons. **helping**
7. My favorite airplane is the P-51. **linking**
8. I have been waiting to go to the airshow. **helping**
9. Airplanes are used by the military and civilians. **helping**
10. The Blue Angels is the U.S. Navy's famous flying team. **linking**
11. Playing flying games on the computer is a hobby of mine. **linking**
12. Inventors have been building flying machines for a long time. **helping**

Page 36

Sweet Tooth

Forms of the verbs *do* and *have* can be used as main verbs or
helping verbs. Helping verbs are added to the front of another
verb and "help" it complete an action.
main verb: I do my work
I had a snack.
helping verb: I do try to eat well.
I have eaten an entire cake.
Note: Don't use *of* when you mean to say *have*.
They should of known her better. (incorrect)
They should have known her better. (correct)

Write **main** or **helping** on the line to tell how the underlined verb in each sentence is used.

1. Mom <u>did</u> tell me to stop eating sweets. **helping**
2. Maybe I should not <u>have</u> had that second donut. **helping**
3. Kate <u>had</u> a new recipe. **main**
4. I <u>did</u> the dinner dishes. **main**
5. Mike <u>does</u> have a weakness for chocolate. **helping**
6. Betsy <u>has</u> liked caramel in the past. **helping**
7. I <u>have</u> four different kinds of gum. **main**
8. Dad <u>does</u> tell me not to eat so much candy. **helping**
9. I <u>did</u> the most eating. **main**
10. Becky <u>has</u> eaten too much food. **helping**

On the line, show how to correct the verbs in each sentence. Not all sentences are incorrect.
Example: I having a good time. I am having a good time.

1. Who done the most work? **Who has done the most work?**
2. We having several cupcakes. **We are having several cupcakes.**
3. This chocolate has a peculiar taste. _____
4. I have did something nice for him. **I have done something nice for him.**
5. He should of saved me some pie. **He should have saved me some pie.**
6. Charlie is having a cookie-tasting party. _____
7. Kate and Mike have did me a favor. **Kate and Mike have done me a favor.**
8. Those nut clusters would have been a good choice. _____

Page 37

Hot Wheels

The **perfect tenses** communicate a sense of continuing action.
The **present tense** shows action begun in the past and completed
in the present. It is formed by adding *has* or *have* to the past
participle.
Dave has passed his road test.
His friends have congratulated him.
The **past perfect tense** shows action begun and completed in the
past. It is formed by adding *had* to the past participle.
He had practiced hard all summer.
The **future perfect tense** shows action begun in the past or
present that will be completed in the future. It is formed by
adding *will have* to the present participle.
Dave will have gotten a new car by next winter.

Show the tense of the perfect verb in each sentence by writing **PR** (present), **P** (past), or **F** (future)
on the line.

PR 1. Kim has left the keys in the car.
F 2. The car will have been stolen by the time we get back.
PR 3. They have scolded her for her carelessness.
P 4. She had worked hard all summer to earn money for the car.
PR 5. Kim has always been rather forgetful.

Copy each sentence, using the tense of the verb shown in parentheses.
1. Our club (collect, present perfect) one-hundred model cars.
Our club has collected one-hundred model cars.
2. Michelle (drive, present perfect) her first car.
Michelle has driven her first car.
3. The new brakes (last, present perfect) all winter.
The new brakes have lasted all winter.
4. She (save, past perfect) all year to buy a convertible.
She had saved all year to buy a convertible.
5. Mandy (buy, future tense) the car by the time we see her.
Mandy will have bought the car by the time we see her.

Page 38

Water World

The **progressive tense** of a verb shows action that is in progress. The present
progressive tense shows action that is going on now. It is formed by adding
a present tense form of *be* (am, is, are) to the present participle (-ing).
I am diving into the pool.
The **past progressive tense** shows action that was in progress in the past.
It is formed by adding a past tense form of *be* (was or were) to the present
participle (-ing).
I was planning to swim.
Note: The present participle is formed by adding *-ing* to the present tense of
a verb. If a verb ends in a silent *e* (advise), the *e* is usually dropped
(advising). If a one-syllable verb ends in a single vowel followed by a
single consonant (cut), the final consonant is often doubled (cutting).

Underline the verb and write whether it is in the present or past progressive tense.
1. We <u>were racing</u> for the championship. **past**
2. My parents <u>are watching</u> from the bleachers. **present**
3. The relay race <u>was taking</u> the most time. **past**
4. You <u>are swimming</u> the fastest. **present**
5. I <u>am floating</u> in the ocean. **present**
6. The synchronized swimmers <u>were moving</u> elegantly. **past**
7. Swimming <u>is becoming</u> my favorite activity. **present**
8. The team <u>was winning</u>. **past**
9. I <u>am starting</u> my dive. **present**
10. My pool toys <u>are floating</u> away. **present**

Write five original sentences using the verb and the progressive tense shown in parentheses.
1. (run, past progressive) **Answers will vary.**
2. (speak, past progressive) _____
3. (go, present progressive) _____
4. (paint, past progressive) _____
5. (chew, present progressive) _____

Page 39

IF87132 *Grammar*

Dear Diary

A **pronoun** is a word that takes the place of a noun. Personal pronouns indicate the speaker (first person), the one spoken to (second person), or the one spoken about (third person).

Singular	Plural
I, me, my, mine	we, us, our, ours
you, your, yours	you, your, yours
he, him, his, she her, hers, it, its	they, them, their, theirs

Circle the personal pronouns in the following diary entry.

Dear Diary,

(You) will never believe the day (I) had today. (Our) team played against the best soccer team in the state in the tournament game. Everyone on (their) team was big and fast. (They) have been undefeated all season, but so have (we). When (we) started to play (I) was pretty nervous. (It) turned out to be a great game! (My) best friend, Joe, was (our) goalie, and (he) played really well. Only one ball got past (him). (His) foot slipped and (he) just couldn't stop (it). Sam, (my) other friend, scored the final goal. (She) was totally excited since (it) was (her) first goal of the entire season. Wow, what a game for (us). (We) beat (them) 5–1, and now the championship trophy is all (ours).

Page 40

Together at Last

Contractions are formed by combining two words.
An apostrophe takes the place of letters that have been left out.
I + am = I'm

Write the contraction for each pair of words below.

1. we + had = **we'd**
2. they + are = **they're**
3. it + is = **it's**
4. he + has = **he's**
5. they + have = **they've**
6. you + are = **you're**
7. it + will = **it'll**
8. she + is = **she's**
9. we + are = **we're**
10. they + will = **they'll**
11. I + have = **I've**
12. they + are = **they're**
13. I + will = **I'll**
14. it + will = **it'll**
15. she + has = **she's**
16. you + have = **you've**

In each sentence below, replace the underlined words with the correct contraction and write it on the line following the sentence.

1. I have always wanted to meet you. **I've**
2. I think they will go to school together. **they'll**
3. She would like to have a best friend. **she'd**
4. We are going to buy a tandem bike. **we're**
5. Please don't tell me you have decided to leave. **you've**
6. He has found his soulmate. **he's**
7. It is a bicycle with two seats. **it's**
8. We will always be friends. **we'll**
9. They have been married for fifty years. **they've**
10. I am waiting for the woman of my dreams. **I'm**

Page 41

Emergency Preparations

A **subject pronoun** replaces a subject noun in a sentence.
Marybeth closed the windows before the storm.
She closed the windows before the storm.

In each of the following sentences, underline the subject noun. Then, rewrite the sentence and replace the subject noun with a subject pronoun.

1. A storm was coming to the little town soon.
   It was coming to the little town soon.
2. Maxwell searched for a flashlight and batteries.
   He searched for a flashlight and batteries.
3. Cameron found the battery-operated radio.
   He found the battery-operated radio.
4. Maxwell and Cameron took cover in the basement.
   They took cover in the basement.
5. Fortunately, a stash of pillows and blankets was nearby.
   Fortunately, it was nearby.
6. Candles, matches, and jugs of fresh water were stored in a box under the bench too.
   They were stored in a box under the bench too.
7. The boys could hear the wind whipping.
   They could hear the wind whipping.
8. Lightning flashed outside the basement window.
   It flashed outside the basement window.

Page 42

Classroom Clean-up

An **object pronoun** replaces the object of a sentence. The direct object tells what or whom receives the action of the verb.
Mrs. Ophoff's class cleaned the room well.
Mrs. Ophoff's class cleaned it well.

In each of the following sentences, cross out the direct object and replace it with an appropriate pronoun.

1. Toby sharpened ~~the pencils.~~ **them**
2. Kate helped ~~Susie and Tina~~ hang up art projects. **them**
3. Mrs. Ophoff cleaned ~~the erasers~~ outside. **them**
4. Some girls helped ~~Mrs. Ophoff~~ by passing out the papers. **her**
5. Paula won ~~the prize~~ for the cleanest desk. **it**
6. Lucas washed ~~the blackboard~~ with water. **it**
7. Stephen offered to help ~~Ivan.~~ **him**
8. Jeffrey straightened ~~all the books on the bookshelf.~~ **them**
9. Jim and Betsy emptied ~~the trash cans.~~ **them**
10. Jason and Sharon fed ~~the hamster.~~ **it**
11. DeShawn watered ~~the plants.~~ **them**
12. Janie washed ~~the tops of the desks.~~ **them**
13. Raquel put away ~~the math game.~~ **it**
14. Carlos and Sonja cleaned out ~~the lockers.~~ **them**
15. Chin swept ~~the floor.~~ **it**
16. Manuel washed ~~the windows.~~ **them**

Page 43

A Trampoline Tale

> Singular pronouns replace singular nouns, and plural pronouns replace plural nouns.
> *singular:* **She** did flips on the trampoline.
> *plural:* **They** jumped on the trampoline.

Underline each pronoun in the following story. Write S over the pronoun if it is singular; write P over the pronoun if it is plural.

    My friends and I like to jump on the trampoline. My parents bought it for me and my sister for our birthdays. It is in the corner of our backyard in the shade. We usually take turns practicing flips and jumps. Dan and Rebekah like to jump with me. They have been working on their flips. Dan can do a high single flip, but he can't beat Rebekah. She is able to do a double flip without any trouble. I don't mean to boast, but I can top both of them. My specialty is a little more complicated. It is a backward double flip! Rebekah told me that she is going to practice her back flips today. Dan said he doesn't even want to try back flips. It is going to be a great day of fun for us.

List each different singular and plural pronoun you found.

SINGULAR		PLURAL
my	me	our
I	he	we
it	she	they
		their
		us

Write the correct pronoun (singular or plural) to replace the underlined word on the line after each sentence.
1. David and I love to jump on the trampoline. *it*
2. The trampoline was given as a gift. *it*
3. Janie gave the tramp to me and Rebekah. *us*
4. Maurice can do a double back flip with a twist. *he*
5. Don't try to get Mom and Dad to jump. *them*
6. Tania likes to show off for her friends. *she*

Page 44

A Word from Our Sponsors

> An **antecedent** is a word for which a pronoun stands. Use singular pronouns with singular antecedents and plural pronouns with plural antecedents.
> *A good advertisement will sell its product. (singular)*
> *Many companies advertise their products on T.V. (plural)*

In each of the following advertisements, underline the pronoun and draw an arrow to the antecedent.

Tuffy's Taffy stretches long and it tastes great!

Feed your puppy Perfect Pup food and he will be a perfectly healthy puppy.

Jackie's Life is now playing at theaters near you, and everyone will want to experience its magic.

Try Tony's Temporary Tattoos; they are easy to use and lots of fun for everyone.

Reach Sports Gear makes quality gear for all athletes wishing to reach their goals.

Famous supermodel, Sandra A. Mazing, wears Glossy Lips lipgloss because she knows a beautiful smile is important.

Buy a pack of Carver's tasty dry-roasted peanuts; you'll love them!

Pete's Party Pizza will make your party last on and on because no one can stop eating it.

Page 45

My Friend and Me

> A **verb** must agree with the **pronoun** in the subject part of the sentence.
> *He runs. (singular)*
> *They run. (plural)*

In each of the following sentences, circle the verb that agrees with the subject pronoun.

1. I (like, likes) my best friend a lot, but we (enjoy, enjoys) different things.

2. For instance, after school I (prefer, prefers) to have a snack and watch T.V., but he always (shoot, shoots) hoops in the driveway.

3. On Saturday morning, all the neighbor kids and I (meet, meets) to play soccer, but my friend (sleep, sleeps) in late.

4. Most people, including myself, love pizza, but he (hate, hates) it.

5. I ask him, "Why do you (wear, wears) that weird hat?"

6. He just (ignore, ignores) me.

7. We (know, knows) it doesn't matter that we're so different because we (is, are) best friends.

Write a sentence for each of these pronouns. Use each pronoun as the subject of the sentence and make sure the verb agrees with it.

(he) 1. Answers will vary.

(it) 2. _____

(they) 3. _____

(we) 4. _____

(she) 5. _____

(you) 6. _____

Page 46

Baby Sitters at Your Service

> Do not use an object pronoun as the subject of a sentence.
> In a sentence with a compound subject, it is incorrect to put the pronoun *I* before the noun.
> *Me is glad you are here. (incorrect)*
> *I am glad you are here. (correct)*
> *Me and Jake play softball. (incorrect)*
> *Jake and I play softball. (correct)*

In each of the following sentences, circle the correct word or pair of words in the parentheses.

1. (Me, I) can baby-sit for you.
2. My friends and (me, I) took a baby-sitting course last summer.
3. The projects we did were very helpful for (me, I).
4. (I, me) made a baby-sitting kit to bring to your home.
5. Your kids and (me, I) will read books and play games together.
6. You can count on (me, I) to be responsible and trustworthy.
7. If you would like references, (me, I) can provide them.
8. (Me, I) believe I will do a wonderful job.
9. (I and you, You and I) can baby-sit together.
10. The money could be divided between (me and you, you and me).
11. (The children and I, I and the children) would like your help.
12. (You and I, You and me) would make a great baby-sitting team!

Page 47

Let It Snow!

Pronoun homophones are pronouns that sound the same as other words but have different spellings and meanings and function differently in sentences.
These are possessive pronouns: *its, their, your, whose*
These are contractions: *it's, they're, you're, who's*
contraction: *It's a beautiful day!*
pronoun: *Its beauty comes from the bright sunshine.*

Circle the correct pronoun homophone in each of the following sentences.

1. (Its, **It's**) beginning to snow again.
2. (Whose, **Who's**) going sledding with me today?
3. Is (**your**, you're) new sled out in the barn?
4. (**You're**, Your) going to have to wear Grandpa's big boots.
5. I think (their, **they're**) on the back porch.
6. (**Whose**, Who's) stocking cap is this?
7. I really like (**its**, it's) fringy tassel.
8. I'm sure Grandma and Grandpa won't mind if we wear (**their**, they're) ski pants.
9. Hurry up, (its, **it's**) going to be dark outside by the time (**your**, you're) ready.
10. Grab (**your**, you're) gloves and let's go!
11. We've got to find the sleds. (Their, **They're**) probably hanging in Grandpa's barn.
12. (**Whose**, Who's) that sledding down the hill now?
13. It looks like David and Meagan with (**their**, they're) little brother.
14. This hill is perfect for sledding, and (**its**, it's) blanket of snow will provide a nice soft ride.
15. Let's race down the hill and see (**whose**, who's) sled is the fastest.
16. (Their, **There**) is little doubt that we will be faster.

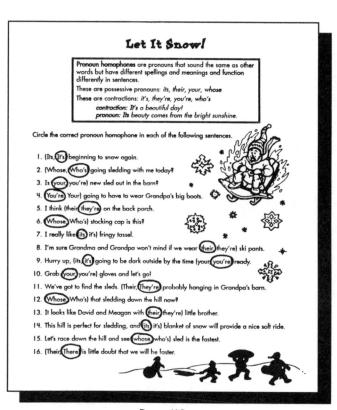

Page 48

Beach or Bust!

A possessive pronoun is one which indicates ownership or possession. Possessive pronouns include: **my, mine, your, yours, his, her, hers, its, our, ours, their, theirs.**
My family loves the beach.

In the following sentences, circle the possessive pronoun and underline the noun it modifies.

1. Look at all (our) stuff.
2. We will never get (our) things into the car.
3. (My) umbrella is far too large.
4. (Your) in-line skates will not fit in the front seat.
5. Is that surfboard (his)
6. Put (his) board on top of the car.
7. You should put (our) cooler in the backseat.
8. What if there's not enough room for (our) bottles of pop?
9. Please don't smash (my) peanut butter and jelly sandwiches.
10. (Her) bicycle will have to stay behind.
11. I have already packed (their) beach bags.
12. Don't forget (their) folding chairs.
13. Make sure you pack the grill with (its) charcoal.
14. That beach blanket is (mine).
15. Remember to bring (your) suntan lotion.
16. I'm going to bring (my) marshmallows.
17. Don't forget (your) graham crackers and chocolate bars.
18. My friends will bring (their) matches.

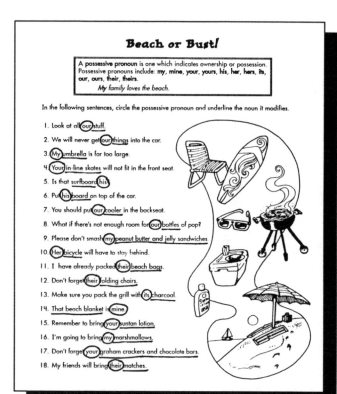

Page 49

The Five W's

An interrogative pronoun is used to begin a question.
Interrogative pronouns include: **who, whom, whose, what,** and **which.**
Who is that masked man?

Circle the interrogative pronouns in each of the following sentences. Then write answers for each of the questions.

1. (Who) is your hero? **Answers will vary.**
2. (What) makes him (or her) so special to you? _____
3. (Which) quality about him (or her) to you admire most? _____
4. With (whom) do you spend a lot of your time? _____
5. (Whose) opinion means the most to you? _____

Fill in the blank with the most appropriate interrogative pronoun.

1. For **whom** were these brownies made?
2. **What** kind are they?
3. **Who** ate some of the frosting?
4. **Which** one do you want?
5. **Whose** brownies are these anyway?

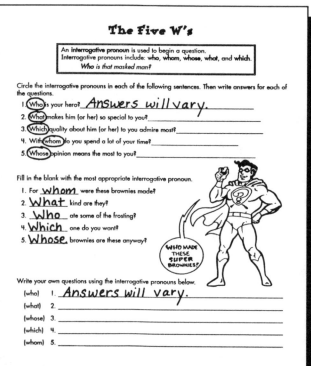

Write your own questions using the interrogative pronouns below.

(who) 1. **Answers will vary.**
(what) 2. _____
(whose) 3. _____
(which) 4. _____
(whom) 5. _____

Page 50

Who?

Who is used as the subject of a verb and **whom** is used as the object. **Who's** is the contraction for *who is* and **whose** is a possessive pronoun.
Who was that masked man?
You are waiting for whom?
Who's making lunch for us today?
Whose sandwich is this?

In each of the following sentences, circle the correct word.

1. (Who's), Whose) on the phone?
2. To (who, (whom)) are you sending the package?
3. (Who's, (Whose)) sticky mess is this?
4. For (who, (whom)) is he waiting?
5. (Who) Whom) ate the last meatball?
6. I have been wondering (who's, (whose)) stinky socks these are.
7. Do you know (who, whom) is having a birthday today?
8. The cat of (who, (whom)) we speak is named Lola.
9. (Who's, (Whose)) yellow raincoat are you wearing?
10. We've been waiting all day to find out (who) whom) the winner is.
11. I appreciate my sister, to (who, (whom)) I tell all my secrets.
12. The author, (who's, (whose)) book you are reading, will sign autographs this afternoon.
13. (Who) Whom) would like a hot fudge sundae?
14. For (who, (whom)) did you sing that love song?
15. Can you remember (who, whom) won the Stanley Cup in 1998?
16. We met a man (who's, (whose)) hair was bright green!

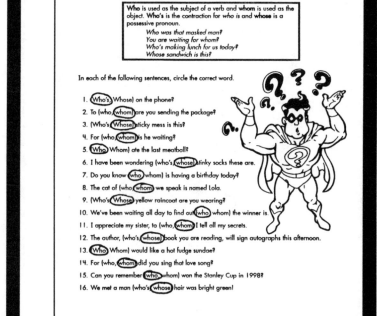

Page 51

115

IF87132 *Grammar*

We Love a Parade

An **indefinite pronoun** is one which gives an approximate number or quantity. It does not tell exactly how many or how much. Some indefinite pronouns include *many, more, fewer, some, several, all,* and *each*. These pronouns often act as adjectives.
The big parade enticed many people downtown.

Circle each indefinite pronoun in the sentences below.

1. (Many) people line the streets to watch the parade.
2. Once the parade begins (several) marching bands perform for the crowd.
3. (Each) band member marches to the cadence of the drum.
4. Usually, a (few) clowns ride their unicycles.
5. (All) of the children stand close to the street to get a closer look.
6. (Some) people in the parade toss candy to the children.
7. The big kids often catch (more) candy than the little ones.
8. A (few) fire trucks join in the fun.
9. It seems that (every) year there are (more) floats than the year before.
10. The parade is great fun for (each) person who participates.
11. (Anyone) can join in the fun.
12. (Both) children and adults work to creat floats.
13. When work is going on (most) people are enthusiastic.
14. A (few) happy people make the whole crew work better.

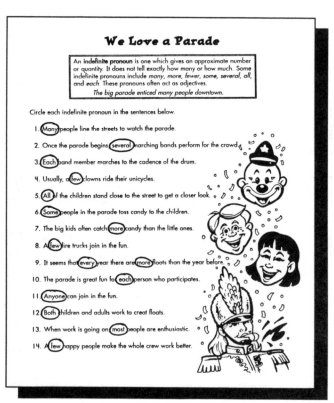

Page 52

For Me?

A **reflexive pronoun** reflects the action of the verb back to the subject.

	singular	plural
first	myself	ourselves
second	yourself	yourselves
third	herself, himself, itself	themselves

The winners congratulated themselves.

Underline the reflexive pronoun in each sentence. Then, circle the noun or pronoun to which the reflexive pronoun refers.

1. (The children) treated themselves to ice cream.
2. (They) timed themselves during the race.
3. (Mary) dressed herself for school.
4. (We) introduced ourselves to the new student.
5. Did (you) make this yourself?

If the reflexive pronoun in each sentence below is used incorrectly, circle it and write the correct reflexive pronoun on the line. If the sentence is correct, write **correct.**

1. I told myself it must be a lie. **correct**
2. We reminded (ourself) of the time. **ourselves**
3. Did she blame (herselves) for the accident? **herself**
4. Some artists have painted (theirselves). **themselves**
5. She bought herself a new dress. **correct**
6. The naughty dog helped itself to some apple pie. **correct**
7. He asked (hisself) what to do. **himself**
8. Did you take that piece of cake for (yourselves), David? **yourself**
9. Please control yourself. **correct**
10. Betsy and Sara took (theirselves) out to a movie. **themselves**

Page 53

Piles of Puckering Pickles

Adjectives are words that describe nouns.
The fuzzy little bumblebee buzzed about the fragrant flowers.

Circle all the adjectives in the pickle advertisement. Write ten more adjectives, one in each pickle.

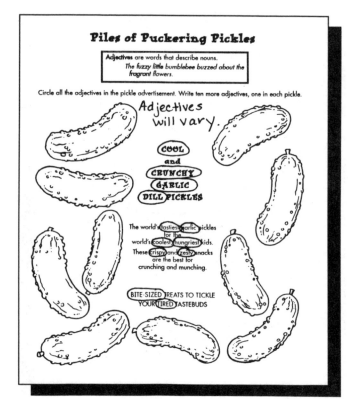

Adjectives will vary.

COOL
and
CRUNCHY
GARLIC
DILL PICKLES

The world's (tastiest) (garlic) pickles for the world's (coolest) (hungriest) kids. These (crispy) and (zesty) snacks are the best for crunching and munching.

(BITE-SIZED) TREATS TO TICKLE YOUR (TIRED) TASTEBUDS

Page 54

That's Corny

An **adjective** modifies a noun or pronoun. It gives specific information by telling *what kind, how many,* or *which one.*
purple cow
thirteen footprints
that creep

In each of the following sentences, circle the adjectives.

1. (Tall) cornstalks grow during the (hot) (summer) months.
2. (That) (Indian) corn is extremely colorful.
3. We like to pop (yellow) corn because it puffs up big and fluffy.
4. Some people like to eat (caramel) corn, but I don't.
5. Sometimes Mom cooks one (jumbo-sized) can of (creamed) corn for (Sunday) dinner.
6. Still, I prefer (juicy) corn on the cob.
7. In (art) class, we made these (corn husk) dolls.
8. Corn was first used by (North) and (South) Americans.
9. Grandma bakes (fluffy) cornbread whenever she serves her (spicy) (Texan) chili.
10. A (fat) and (crispy) corndog is the (perfect) treat at the (county) fair.
11. Cows munch on (dry) corn at mealtimes.
12. (Most) corn is grown in the (prolific) Corn Belt of the United States.

Write three original sentences using the adjectives given.

1. (green) **Answers will vary.**
_____

2. (those) _____
_____

3. (rusty) _____
_____

Page 55

IF87132 *Grammar*

Forty Feathered Falcons

An **adjective** modifies a noun or pronoun. It gives specific information by telling *what kind, how many,* or *which one.*
yellow buttercup
forty ferrets
that thorn

In front of each adjective-noun pair, write 1 for *what kind,* 2 for *how many,* or 3 for *which one.*

2 two teaspoons
1 poor pilot
2 nine nuns
3 that man
1 blue balloon
2 eighty eggs
1 brown bear
1 strong sailor
1 fast footwork
3 this week
1 mean muskrat
2 one wish

1 frantic Fred
1 pink posies
1 growing garden
1 jade jewelry
1 opposite opinions
3 these things
2 four friends
2 some sneakers
3 an apple
1 crazy clowns
1 vivacious Vivian
3 those thugs

Page 56

Take Me Out to the Ballgame

A, an, and *the* are the three most commonly used articles. *A* and *an* are **indefinite** articles, referring to any one of a class of nouns. *A* is used before words that begin with consonants. Use *an* before words that begin with vowels. *The* is **definite** and refers to a specific noun.
a shower
an apple
the dog

Use either *a, an,* or *the* to complete the sentences below.

Baseball is **an** All-American sport. It is played with **a** leather-covered ball and **a** wooden or metal bat. **A** batter swings and hits **the** ball across **a** diamond-shaped field. Then he begins to run **the** bases. If he is able to run all **the** way back to home plate, where he started, he has scored **a** homerun. **An** outfielder or **an** infielder tries to catch **the** ball and stop **the** runner. In **an** inning, each team is allowed three outs. **The** game is finished at **the** end of nine innings.

Circle the correct article in each sentence below.

1. Everyone has to have a (an) hotdog.
2. Many people try to catch (a) an homerun ball.
3. Most root for (a, the) home team and hope for (a) an win.
4. (A, An) umpire calls balls and strikes from behind (a, the) catcher.
5. I like to sing (a, an) enthusiastic round of "Take Me Out to the Ballgame."
6. Before we leave, we always try to get (a, an) autograph from at least one player.

Page 57

Around the World

Proper nouns are the specific names of people, places, or things. **Proper adjectives** are formed from these proper nouns. They usually begin with capital letters.
North American people
Canadian bacon

Underline all of the adjectives. Write a P above the proper adjectives and a C above the common (regular) ones.

P Italian spaghetti
C Swiss chocolate
C sumo wrestling
P African safari
C friendly dog

C hot cocoa
C fun fiesta
P Irish pub
P Dutch dance
C flour tortillas

C green shamrocks
C wooden shoes
P Mexican border
C tall giraffes
P lively polka

P Polish sausage
C sausage meatballs
P Japanese kimono
P Spanish rice
P English setter

In the following sentences, capitalize the proper adjectives.

1. On Saturday mornings, we usually have French toast.
2. Mom always buys Idaho potatoes at the supermarket.
3. For my birthday, I had Chinese food and chocolate cake.
4. Dad's spicy Texan chili is great on a cold day.
5. The restaurant on the corner serves a great Greek salad with anchovies.
6. I love to eat Maine lobster dipped in melted butter.
7. Grandma's German potato salad is too sour for my taste.
8. Her Belgian waffles are heavenly, though.
9. We enjoy spicy Latin American foods.
10. One of the best desserts in the world is New York cheesecake.

Page 58

Rocky, the Wonder Dog

There are three forms, or degrees, of adjectives that are used in comparison. The **positive** degree is used to describe one item or person. The **comparative** degree is used when making a comparison between two items or people. The **superlative** degree is used when comparing more than two items or people.
positive: George is crafty.
comparative: George is craftier than Roger.
superlative: George is the craftiest of the three boys.

Complete the adjective chart.

POSITIVE	COMPARATIVE	SUPERLATIVE
loud	louder	loudest
quick	quicker	quickest
tardy	tardier	tardiest
stinky	stinkier	stinkiest
wise	wiser	wisest
sweet	sweeter	sweetest
angry	angrier	angriest
bright	brighter	brightest
strong	stronger	strongest
green	greener	greenest

In the following sentences, underline the comparative and superlative adjectives. If the adjective is comparative, write C in the blank. If it is superlative, write S.

S 1. Rocky is the coolest dog around.
C 2. He has a few white spots on his ears and a bigger spot on his nose.
S 3. Rocky is the strongest member of my family.
S 4. He is the loudest sleeper in my family.
C 5. My dog has a louder snore than I do.
C 6. His coat is softer than any of my aunt's dogs.
C 7. Rocky is a better frisbee catcher than anyone I know.
S 8. He is also the highest jumper.
S 9. And, he is the fastest runner of all my pets.
S 10. Rocky is the smartest dog in the world.

Page 59

IF87132 *Grammar*

Sammy

Adjectives change form to show comparison. The endings **er** and **est** are added, or comparison words such as *more, most, less,* and *least* are used. Do not use comparison words with **er** or **est** words.

Sammy is my most specialest cousin. (incorrect)
Sammy is my most special cousin. (correct)
He is more friendlier than anyone I know. (incorrect)
He is friendlier than anyone I know. (correct)

Circle the correct adjective in each of the following sentences.

1. My cousin Sammy is the (cutest, most cutest) kid!
2. He's only three years old, and he does the (funnier, funniest) things.
3. Sammy is (more fun, most fun) than any other little kids I know.
4. When I push him on the swings he always says, "Push me (faster, more faster), Bailey!"
5. When we play on the merry-go-round, we go (slower, slowest) than the big kids.
6. Usually, I carry him home on my back because it's (quicker, quickest) than having him walk.
7. He says the (craziest, most craziest) things, too.
8. Besides that, Sammy always tells me that I am his (smartest, most smart) cousin.
9. Sammy's hair is even (redder, more redder) than mine.
10. His dimples are the (bigger, biggest) I have ever seen.
11. He has the (most adorable, most adorablest) smile in the whole world.
12. The time we spend together is (more special, most special) to me than just about anything.
13. The day we spend together is (more better, better) than the other days of the week.
14. The time I spend with my other cousins is the (worst, worstest).

Page 60

At the Movies

This, that, these, and *those* are **demonstrative adjectives** that point out a particular person, place, or thing. Use *this* and *these* for things close by and *that* and *those* for things distant in time or space. *This* and *that* are singular. *These* and *those* are plural.

this box at my feet   *these boxes at my feet*
that box in the other   *those boxes in the*
room   *other room*

Circle the most appropriate demonstrative adjective in each sentence below.

1. (These, Those) tickets cost less than the ones for the evening show.
2. Let's get some of (this, that) popcorn over there.
3. I like (this, that) theater better than the one across town.
4. Grab two of (these, those) seats down in front.
5. (This, That) screen might actually be too close now.
6. Let's move back to (these, those) seats behind us.
7. (This, That) movie is pretty good.
8. And (these, those) seats are better, aren't they?

Write a demonstrative adjective before each of the following objects.

these papers (near)   **that** dog (far)
that globe (far)   **this** rollercoaster (near)
this hand (near)   **those** shoes (far)
that hair style (far)   **these** dentures (near)
this candy (near)   **those** students (far)
those athletes (far)   **this** football field (near)
this city (near)   **that** goat (far)
that mall (far)   **these** movie stars (near)

Page 61

A Good Job Well Done

Good and *bad* are adjectives. *Well* and *badly* are adverbs.

Matthew made a good shot.
A bad pass messed up the play.
Matthew played well.
The ball was passed badly.

In each of the following sentences, circle the correct modifier in the parentheses.

1. Miko is a (good, well) artist.
2. She paints nature scenes especially (good, well).
3. She doesn't do too (bad, badly) on portraits either.
4. Her paintings of the ocean at sunrise are really (good, well).
5. Miko says she paints (good, well) when she is outside.
6. I would like to paint as (good, well) as she.

1. Stanley plays the guitar (good, well).
2. I must admit that I play the guitar very (bad, badly).
3. He has a (good, well) guitar too.
4. The music he writes is (good, well).
5. His lyrics aren't (bad, badly) written.
6. Unfortunately, his voice isn't very (good, well).

1. I try not to get (bad, badly) grades.
2. Right now I am doing pretty (good, well) in writing.
3. I had (good, well) comments on my last story.
4. I know I can write better if I practice (good, well).
5. I think I will do (well, good) on my next paper.
6. If I do (bad, badly) I may have to spend less time playing.

Page 62

The Toothache

An **adverb** is a word that modifies a verb, an adjective, or another adverb. Adverbs indicate *time, place,* or *manner.*

time: brushes daily
place: flosses here
manner: gargles noisily

In the following sentences, circle the adverbs and indicate if they are time (T), place (P), or manner (M).

M   1. My tooth ached (badly).
T   2. Mom (immediately) decided that I had to go to the dentist.
P   3. Before I knew it, I was waiting (there) in Dr. Chong's office.
M   4. The nauseating smell of antiseptic (really) bothered me.
M   5. I tapped my finger (anxiously) on the chair.
T   6. I (now) noticed a man had fallen asleep while he waited for the dentist.
M   7. A woman across the room (silently) read a magazine.
T   8. (Finally) the nurse called my name.
P   9. I stood and walked (in).
M   10. At that moment, I felt (nauseatingly) sick to my stomach.
T   11. (Soon) the nurse directed me to a dental chair.
T   12. (Instantly) the dentist arrived wearing a mask and plastic gloves.
M   13. He was smiling (broadly) behind his mask.
P   14. "Let's take a look (here)," he said.
P   15. I sat (there) hoping he would not yank out my tooth.
T   16. I (always) dread going to that dentist's chair.

Page 63

IF87132 *Grammar*

Late Kate

An adverb is a word that modifies a verb, an adjective, or another adverb. **Adverbs of time** answer the questions *when* or *how often*.

*We like to go to the movies **sometimes**.*

Use the adverbs of time from the Word Bank to modify the verbs and complete the sentences below. **Note:** You will not use all the words in the bank.

Word Bank				
never	eventually	next	usually	often
then	frequently	first	always	finally
later	soon	seldom	today	constantly

Late Kate was **never** on time for anything. **Usually** she was very late for everything. Kate **often** arrived at school after the tardy bell had rung. **Constantly** she made her friends wait for her. "Hurry, hurry, slow-poke Kate," they **always** said.

Eventually Kate's friends had waited long enough. **Today** they decided to teach her a lesson that they hoped she would never forget. **First** Kate's friends sent her an invitation to a special party given in her honor. They set to work, and **soon** the room was decorated with streamers and bright colored balloons. **Finally** they hung a banner from one end of the room to the next. **Then** all of Kate's friends went home. Sure enough, Kate arrived **later**, but she was sad to discover only a quiet room and a banner that read "Sorry you are late Kate. You missed all the fun!"

Use the three adverbs from the Word Bank that were not used in the above sentences to write sentences of your own. Be sure the adverb modifies a verb.

1. next _____ Sentences
2. seldom _____ will
3. frequently or constantly _____ vary.

Page 64

A Cinderella Story

Adverbs of place answer the question *where*. They usually modify verbs.
*Cinderella's stepsisters were always **nearby** with work for her to do.*

In the following sentences, circle the adverbs that answer the question *where* and underline the verbs they modify.

1. Cinderella was sent upstairs to live in the attic.
2. Mice lived there too.
3. Spiderwebs hung everywhere in her dismal room.
4. Sadness and gloom threatened inside.
5. But, the sun shone outside her window.
6. Cinderella's stepmother and stepsisters stayed downstairs.
7. Cinderella could come down only to cook and clean for them.
8. When they were away, she would sit beside the fire.
9. As the fire blazed, her mice friends searched nearby for some crumbs.
10. Here she could dream of faraway places and happy endings.
11. Cinderella longed to meet her prince at the ball and run away with him.
12. Her wonderful fairy godmother arranged to get Cinderella there.
13. And so, Cinderella ran away with her prince.

Fill in an adverb that answers *where* in each of the following sentences.
Answers will vary.
1. The sparkling carriage stopped _____ the castle.
2. Cinderella and the prince danced _____ a glittering chandelier.
3. They strolled _____ the twinkling stars.
4. The prince looked _____ for Cinderella.

Page 65

The Pool Party

Adverbs of manner answer the questions *how* or *in what manner*. They often end in *-ly*.
*Put on your swimsuit **quickly**.*

In each of the following sentences, circle the adverb of manner and underline the verb it modifies.

1. Mr. Peter's fifth grade class rushed excitedly to the pool area.
2. The clear blue water sparkled invitingly in the sunshine.
3. Quickly everyone prepared to jump into the pool.
4. Suddenly Carlos yelled, "Wait everybody!"
5. "Let's all jump together," he continued.
6. Mr. Peters offered to count aloud to three and yell "Go."
7. All the students stood expectantly around the pool.
8. When everyone was ready, Mr. Peters loudly shouted, "1, 2, 3,...GO!"
9. Twenty-nine students leaped simultaneously into the cold pool water.
10. Together they created a huge burst of water.
11. Everyone hollered happily and splashed one another.
12. While they celebrated, Mr. Peters totally surprised them by doing an enormous cannonball off the diving board.

Fill in an adverb that answers *how* or *in what manner* in each of the following sentences.
Answers will vary.
1. Patrick _____ dove off the high board.
2. Mary Ann _____ stuck a toe into the cold pool water.
3. Chin ran _____ toward the pool and did a belly flop.
4. "Bombs away!" Chin yelled _____.

Page 66

Positive, Comparative, Superlative

There are three forms, or degrees, of adverbs that are used in comparison. The **positive degree** is used when describing one action. The **comparative degree** is used when comparing two actions. The **superlative degree** is used when comparing more than two actions. When an adverb ends in *ly*, it usually compares by adding *more* or *most*.

Positive	Comparative	Superlative
low	lower	lowest
carefully	more carefully	most carefully

Write the missing adverbs in the chart.

POSITIVE	COMPARATIVE	SUPERLATIVE
sweetly	more sweetly	most sweetly
late	later	latest
quietly	more quietly	most quietly
soon	sooner	soonest
clearly	more clearly	most clearly
safely	more safely	most safely
rapidly	more rapidly	most rapidly
hard	harder	hardest
high	higher	highest
easily	more easily	most easily
quickly	more quickly	most quickly
powerfully	more powerfully	most powerfully
deep	deeper	deepest
gracefully	more gracefully	most gracefully
tragically	more tragically	most tragically
playfully	more playfully	most playfully

Page 67

'Round and About

A preposition is a word that relates a noun or a pronoun to another word in the sentence. Prepositions indicate a relationship between separate things.

My book bag is near the door.
His shoes are on his feet.

Familiarize yourself with several prepositions by filling in the word search puzzle. Look ↓↑ ←→ ↗↘. A few two-letter prepositions may appear more than once.

Word Bank

during	to	of	past	for	with
onto	by	through	beyond	beside	around
in	near	between	over	about	outside
until	from	since	off	after	below
under	before				

Page 68

One Hump or Two?

A prepositional phrase is a group of words that begins with a preposition and ends with the object of the preposition. A preposition is a word or group of words that shows a relationship between the words in a sentence.

There are several different kinds of camels.

Underline each prepositional phrase in the following sentences.

1. Camels are animals that have humps on their backs.
2. A large lump of fat is located inside the hump.
3. A dromedary is a camel with just one hump.
4. Some animals without humps also belong to the camel family.
5. Many camels live in the African and Arabian deserts.
6. Others live in the South American mountains.
7. The camels' huge feet help them to walk over hot desert sand.
8. They have broad bony ridges above each eye to shield them from the sun.
9. A camel can shut its nostrils to keep sand out of its nose.
10. Camels have large eyes on the sides of their heads.
11. The camel's hump is a place for storing fat, but not water.
12. A thirsty camel can drink more than fifty gallons of water in one day.
13. Camels do not need to drink water during cooler weather.
14. A camel can travel long distances across hot deserts.
15. Today, camels are still used by nomads.
16. In desert areas, camels pull plows and turn water wheels to irrigate fields.
17. On extremely hot days, a camel keeps cool by resting in a shady place.
18. The long fur of some camels is good for weaving into cloth.

Page 69

Camp Cooleewowa

The noun or pronoun used as the **object of the preposition** follows the preposition. The object and the preposition form what is called the **prepositional phrase**. Often, a prepositional phrase that begins a sentence will be set off by a comma.

Brett fell in the stream.
It seemed very funny to us.
Instead of helping him, we laughed and laughed.

To find the object of the preposition, ask *whom* or *what* after the preposition.

Brett fell in what? the stream
It seemed funny to whom? us
Instead of helping whom? him

Read the paragraphs below. Place parentheses around the prepositional phrases and underline the object of the preposition.

Every summer I go (with my best friend) to Camp Cooleewowa. It's a really cool place. Ten campers and two counselors stay (in each cabin). We put our sleeping bags (on the bunk beds) and slide our suitcases (under the bottom bunk). There is a fireplace (at one end of the room). Each night, we start a fire (in the fireplace) to warm the cabin before bedtime. Everything is perfect, (except for the bathrooms); we use stinky outhouses!

The camp is located (on the northern side) of Lake Coolee. Every morning we get to go canoeing (across the lake). (In the afternoon) we dive off the docks (into the crystal-clear lake water). (After dinner) all the campers gather to play games like volleyball, basketball, and soccer. (Before bedtime) everyone meets (around the fire pit) (on the beach). The bright fire burning (in the darkness) gets us telling spooky stories and silly camp songs.

(At the end of an exciting week) we all go home knowing that we will come back again next summer (for another week of Cooleewowa fun).

Page 70

Fruity Flavors

A prepositional phrase is a group of words that shows how two words or ideas are related to each other. Like a one-word adjective, an **adjective prepositional phrase** modifies a noun or pronoun.

My favorite fruit in the whole world is the orange.

In the following sentences, underline the adjective prepositional phrases and circle the words being modified.

1. The peaches in the bowl will make a tasty pie.
2. The fruit stand near the corner has quarts of fresh raspberries for sale.
3. The cantaloupe in the refrigerator will be a good bedtime snack.
4. A handful of sliced grapes will sweeten the chicken salad.
5. The bananas on the trees are still not ripe.
6. A big watermelon from the garden will be our dessert.
7. The pineapples of the Hawaiian islands are sweet and juicy.
8. One cherry on top of an ice-cream sundae is just right.
9. One of the oranges next to the salad bowl was as big as a softball.
10. Let's pick the berries along the fence.
11. Pies with a lot of fruit are the best.
12. I love the blueberries from Grandpa's farm.
13. Bananas with very dark spots usually end up in banana bread.
14. The pears from our own pear trees are yellowish-green.
15. Most fruits of any season are flavorful.

Page 71

Bowl-a-thon

Like a one-word adverb, an adverb prepositional phrase usually modifies a verb and may tell *where, how,* or *when* an action takes place. It relates a word or phrase in a sentence to another word or phrase.

We went bowling at the bowling alley.
(where did we go bowling?)
We bowled with our friends cheering us on.
(how did we bowl?)
We went bowling after school.
(when did we go bowling?)

In each of the following sentences, underline the adverb prepositional phrase and circle the verb or verb phrase being modified.

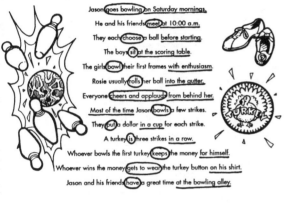

Jason goes bowling on Saturday mornings.
He and his friends meet at 10:00 a.m.
They each choose a ball before starting.
The boys sit at the scoring table.
The girls bowl their first frames with enthusiasm.
Rosie usually rolls her ball into the gutter.
Everyone cheers and applauds from behind her.
Most of the time Jason bowls a few strikes.
They put a dollar in a cup for each strike.
A turkey is three strikes in a row.
Whoever bowls the first turkey keeps the money for himself.
Whoever wins the money gets to wear the turkey button on his shirt.
Jason and his friends have a great time at the bowling alley.

Page 72

Art in a Box

A prepositional phrase contains a preposition and a noun or pronoun acting as the object of the preposition. These phrases can act as *adjectives* or *adverbs.*

Follow the directions on this page.
(adjective—describes which directions)
Follow the directions with care.
(adverb—describes how to follow)

In the following sentences, underline the prepositional phrases. On each line, write ADJ if it is an adjective phrase or ADV if it is an adverb phrase. Then complete the picture.

ADV 1. Add hair to the stick person.
ADJ 2. Color the cat next to the person black.
ADV 3. Draw a silver lining around each cloud.
ADV 4. Put a flower on the middle stem.
ADJ 5. Sketch a bird flying between the clouds.
ADV 6. Create green grass beneath the cat and the stick person.
ADV 7. Put a butterfly net in the stick person's right hand.
ADV 8. Make butterflies flying about the net.
ADJ 9. Give the flower at the far right a smiley face.
ADJ 10. Color the sky behind the scene light blue.
ADV 11. Draw two eyes and a smile on the stick person's face.
ADV 12. Add a tail to the cat's left side.

Page 73

Happy Trails

Some words can be used as prepositions or as adverbs. An adverb will not have an object as a preposition does.
preposition: The wagon traveled down the mountain.
adverb: The rain came down and soaked the wagon.

Write **preposition** or **adverb** on the line to show the use of the underlined word in each sentence.

1. The horses weren't complaining <u>about</u> the wagons full of hayriders. **preposition**
2. The trees seemed to smile as we passed <u>by</u>. **adverb**
3. The hay kept us warm as we rode <u>beneath</u> the stars. **preposition**
4. Stars seem to shine so brightly when city lights aren't <u>around</u>. **adverb**
5. The sky stretched <u>above</u> as we sang hay-ride songs. **adverb**
6. It felt great sitting <u>beside</u> the fire. **preposition**
7. The horses pulled the wagons <u>along</u> the dusty trail. **preposition**
8. The horses seemed thirsty as they waded <u>across</u> the stream. **preposition**
9. I was a little frightened, but my horse went <u>through</u> just fine. **adverb**
10. Traveling seems more peaceful when you leave your car <u>behind</u>. **adverb**

Change the adverb to a preposition by completing each sentence below.

1. The wagon creaked <u>along</u> **Answers will vary.**
2. We rode <u>past</u> _____
3. Falling stars streaked the sky <u>above</u> _____
4. Happy faces were all <u>around</u> _____
5. Darkness fell <u>outside</u> _____
6. We all gathered <u>around</u> _____
7. Everyone walked <u>along</u> _____
8. We went <u>inside</u> _____
9. The wagon went <u>down</u> _____
10. We all climbed <u>off</u> _____

Page 74

Gosh, Thanks

Interjections are words that express strong feeling or sudden emotion. An interjection may be followed by an exclamation point or a comma. Interjections are more effective when they are not overused.
Wow! What a surprise!
Oh, give me a break.

Choose an interjection from the Word Bank for each of the following sentences.

WORD BANK			
wow	yikes	oh	oops
ouch	phew	eureka	hey
help	well	thanks	yes
ugh	psst	gosh	whew
aha	shh	nonsense	terrific

Answers will vary.

1. _____! I am glad you made the team.
2. _____! I can't lift this by myself.
3. _____, I think I get it now.
4. _____! Please be quiet!
5. _____! That was a close one.
6. _____! That never happened.
7. _____! I really made a mess.
8. _____, that was very nice of you.
9. _____! We've caught you!
10. _____, would you like to come along with us?

Write sentences with the following interjections.
1. Wow! **Answers will vary.**
2. Ouch! _____
3. Phew! _____
4. Eureka! _____
5. Well, _____

Page 75

IF87132 *Grammar*

Page 76

Hockey

An appositive is a noun, pronoun, or noun phrase placed next to, or very near, another noun or pronoun to identify, explain, or rename it.

Wayne Gretsky, a famous hockey player, retired from the New York Rangers in 1999.

In each of the following sentences, underline the appositive and circle the noun it explains. Add commas around the appositives.

1. Hockey, a popular sport, is played in Canada, in the United States of America, and in Europe.
2. Fast-skating Sid, a fair and friendly referee, gives out penalties.
3. Frank drives the zamboni, an ice-smoothing machine, around the rink.
4. Some players wear masks, wire face guards, to protect themselves.
5. Hockey players who are tough athletes, train and practice daily.
6. Hockey may have developed from a game played by Neanderthals, prehistoric humans.
7. Players who participate in fighting may have to spend time at the penalty bench, or penalty box.
8. The goals, net covered structures, stand at each end of the ice.
9. A hat trick, three goals scored by a single player in one game, is a rarity.
10. Players spend time in the penalty box, a glassed-in seating area, after breaking the game's rules.
11. Hockey fans, people of all ages, cheer loudly for their favorite team.
12. Fighting, a frequent occurrence, may result in penalties or expulsion from the game.
13. Icing, flinging the puck from one end of the rink to the other, should be avoided.
14. Gordy Howe, a famous hockey player, played for the Redwings.
15. Before the 1870's, a rubber ball, rather than a puck was used to play hockey.
16. Clarence, the hockey goalie, loves to stop the puck.
17. The NHL teams compete for the ultimate reward, the Stanley Cup.
18. The first professional hockey team was organized in 1903 in Michigan, the home of the Detroit Redwings.

Page 77

Enter at Your Own Risk

Use only one negative when you mean to say no.

*It **doesn't** do **no** good to clean your room if you just get it messy again. (incorrect)*

*It **doesn't** do any good to clean your room if you just get it messy again. (correct)*

Circle the correct word from the pair in parentheses.

1. I can't (ever never) keep my room clean for very long.
2. I recommend that you don't (ever never) enter my room when it is a mess.
3. There isn't (any no) way out of such a disaster area.
4. In fact, you might not (ever never) escape.
5. There just aren't (any no) guarantees for your safety.
6. In fact, we haven't been able to find (anyone no one) who entered last week.
7. There isn't a sign of them (anywhere nowhere).
8. Besides that, I haven't (ever never) found my pet snake in there either.
9. She wasn't (anywhere nowhere) to be seen.
10. Believe me, it doesn't make (any no) sense to go in there if you don't have to.

Enter at Your Own Risk!!

Correct the double negatives in these sentences.

1. We won't do none of your cleaning for you.
   We won't do any of your cleaning for you.
2. I don't want no money to help you clean it.
   I don't want any money to help you clean it.
3. I'm sorry, but I can't do nothing to help you out.
   I'm sorry, but I can't do anything to help you out.
4. There isn't nobody here who will clean your room.
   There isn't anybody here who will clean your room.
5. The maid came, but there wasn't nobody home.
   The maid came, but there wasn't anybody home.
6. There weren't no window cleaner left.
   There wasn't any window cleaner left.

Page 78

Oops!

A **sentence** is a group of words that expresses a complete thought. Sentences must have subjects and predicates. The subject tells whom or what the sentence is about. The predicate tells what the subject is or does.

Emily runs out of school. (sentence)
Yells at her little brother. (not a sentence)

Put a star next to each group of words below that is a sentence.
1. The school bell rang. ★
2. Running out of school.
3. Slipped on a banana peel.
4. Jeff fell on the ground. ★
5. His knee was cut. ★

Draw a vertical line between the subject and the predicate in each sentence below.
1. Shawn | clumsily tripped over a garden rake.
2. The little girl | tumbled down the basement stairs.
3. My dad | bumped his head on the chandelier.
4. The dog | skid on the rug and hit the wall.
5. Melissa | slid on a leaf and fell while in-line skating.

Add words to the groups of words below to make them into complete sentences. Make as many different sentences as you can.
- the exhausted backpackers
- deserted in the mountains
- a scary noise

Answers will vary, but should be in complete sentences.

Page 79

Ice Cream, You Scream!

The **simple subject** is the essential noun of the sentence, not including articles or modifiers. It cannot be left out of a complete subject.

The team won free ice-cream cones.

In each of the following sentences, draw a box around the simple subject.

1. Ice cream tastes great on a hot day.
2. Most people enjoy at least one kind of ice cream.
3. After the soccer game, we went to Cone World for an ice-cream treat.
4. My choice is always the same.
5. I choose chocolate every time.
6. Karla hates chocolate.
7. She gets one dip of bubblegum and one dip of blue moon.
8. Kyle says that is gross!
9. Kyle's favorite is a banana split with a cherry on the top.
10. Once in a while, our coach buys us ice cream.
11. The team always plays better if the ice cream is going to be free.
12. Today we won the playoffs.
13. Our coach bought us jumbo banana splits.
14. Kyle ate so much he says he will never even look at another banana split.
15. Karla got in a food fight with Jack.
16. I hid under a table.
17. The coach told Karla and Jack to help mop the floor.

IF87132 *Grammar*

Grandma Mae

The **complete subject** of a sentence is the noun, pronoun, or group of words acting as a noun that tells who or what the sentence is about. Complete subjects include modifiers such as adjectives or prepositions.

My sweet grandmother knitted a sweater.

Underline the complete subject in each sentence below.

1. My grandma has her own way of doing things.

2. When we go out, she always carries an umbrella.

3. Her hot pink suede shoes are the coolest.

4. Grandma Mae never leaves the house without a hat either.

5. One of her favorite hats has a big floppy brim trimmed with plastic pansies.

6. All of her fingers display huge rings, which Grandma calls her "baubles."

7. Once a month, a hair dresser dyes Grandma Mae's hair purple.

8. I think her hair complements her pink suede shoes nicely.

9. Most of the time, her pet Chihuahua sits in Grandma's big straw purse.

10. Grandma calls her dog Kisses.

11. When we eat at Grandma's house, she makes all our meals into works of art.

12. For dessert, she carves birds out of apples.

13. My mom and dad say Grandma is eccentric.

14. I believe Grandma Mae is the best grandma in the world.

Page 80

A Snowy Home

The **simple predicate** is the verb or verb phrase that tells what the subject is or what it does. It does not include any modifying words. The simple predicate cannot be left out of the complete predicate.

Eskimos create dome-shaped homes out of snow blocks.

In each of the following sentences, draw a box around the simple predicate.

1. Jamie and Dad built an igloo in their backyard.

2. They made the bricks out of snow.

3. After a few hours, the igloo was finished.

4. The snow fell all day long.

5. Dad suggested something adventurous.

6. Dad and Jamie agreed to spend the night in their igloo.

7. Dad cooked beans on the campstove.

8. Jamie poured hot chocolate into mugs.

9. After dinner, Dad told Jamie ghost stories.

10. Before dark, Jamie laid the sleeping bags on top of a blanket inside the igloo.

11. Dad grabbed the flashlights and pillows.

12. At bedtime, they snuggled into their sleeping bags.

13. Of course, Mom worried about them.

14. Still, the winter campers stayed warm all night long in their igloo.

15. They had a great time too.

Page 81

Twice as Nice

The **complete predicate** is the verb or verb phrase, containing all modifiers, that tells what the subject is or what it does.

The twins, Clay and Carla Crawford, were born on July 4, 1990.

In each of the following sentences, underline the complete predicate.

1. My sister and I are twins.

2. Her name is Carla Marie Crawford.

3. My full name is Clayton Maxwell Crawford.

4. Everyone calls me Clay.

5. Our birthday is on the Fourth of July.

6. I was born first.

7. Four minutes later, Carla was born.

8. We are fraternal twins.

9. No one thinks that we look very much alike.

10. Some identical twins dress alike.

11. We do not!

12. We each have our own personalities.

13. Being a twin is okay with me.

14. My sister is pretty cool.

15. We like to play basketball together.

16. Our mom calls us "Double Trouble."

Page 82

Tune Up the Band

The **complete subject** of a sentence tells what or who the sentence is about. The **complete predicate** tells what the subject is or does. Both may be one word or many.

(complete subject) (complete predicate)
Gifted musicians create beautiful music.

In each of the following sentences, underline the complete subject once; underline the complete predicate twice.

The band students made a tremendous racket during their warm-up.

The drum major banged his baton on the ground.

Every drummer beat his drums loudly.

Clarinets squeaked and squawked.

Each one of the flute players practiced a scale.

Ten trombones blared.

Behind them, several tubas boomed.

A pair of cymbals clanged along.

Several saxophones sounded nearby.

Loudest of all, the trumpets blasted with all their might.

All that noise made everyone's ears hurt.

Page 83

Snorkeling in Maui

> A **coordinating conjunction** is a word that joins words or groups of words together. They include: **and, but, or, nor, for, yet,** and **so.** These conjunctions connect words or sentences that are alike.
> *Snorkeling and scuba diving* are great ways to experience marine life firsthand.

Circle the coordinating conjunctions in each of the following sentences.

Brett (and) Kamal went snorkeling in the ocean. They wore masks (and) snorkels (but) no fins. Both of them hoped to see beautiful fish (or) colorful coral, so they swam toward the rocks. The sun overhead was hot (but) the water was clear (and) cool. Diving into the ocean felt refreshing (but) tasting the salty water did not. Brett swam after an interesting school of fish (so) Kamal dove after him. The boys had to decide whether to continue diving (or) return to the boat. When they returned, they discussed the corals (and) tropical fish they had seen. Some snorkelers had seen big sea turtles (but) Brett (and) Kamal had not. They hoped to use their underwater cameras (and) to snap pictures tomorrow. This was not their first snorkeling trip (nor) would it be their last.

Write four sentences using each conjunction noted.

1. (and) Answers will vary.

2. (but) _____

3. (or) _____

4. (so) _____

Page 84

Aesop's Fables

> A **compound subject** consists of two or more subjects joined by a conjunction. These subjects share a verb.
> *Lessons and morals* are taught in Aesop's fables.

In each of the following sentences, circle the conjunction and underline the two subjects it joins.

1. The town mouse (and) the country mouse like their own homes best.
2. The lion (and) the mouse demonstrate the importance of kindness.
3. The monkey (and) the dolphins show how one lie leads to another.
4. The bear (and) the bees learn to control their anger.
5. A hare (and) a tortoise race one another to the finish line.
6. Aesop's cat (and) old rat teach us that wise people don't fall for the same trick twice.
7. The mole (and) his mother tell us how foolish it is to boast.
8. The north wind (and) the sun prove that gentleness and kindness are more powerful than force.

Combine the two sentences by creating a compound subject in each. Use the conjunction noted at the beginning of each sentence. You may need to change the verb to a plural form.

(and) 1. The fifth grade class is studying Aesop's fables. The sixth grade class is studying Aesop's fables.
The fifth and sixth grade classes are studying Aesop's fables.

(or) 2. Joe has the book. Frank has the book.
Joe or Frank has the book.

(and) 3. The boys like the fables. The girls like the fables.
The boys and the girls like the fables.

(or) 4. David will read the fable aloud. Bradley will read the fable aloud.
David or Bradley will read the fable aloud.

(and) 5. Mrs. Davis's class will act out some fables. Mr. Sim's class will act out some fables.
Mrs. Davis's class and Mr. Sims class will act out some fables.

(or) 6. Candace will be a frog. Sandra will be a frog.
Candace or Sandra will be a frog.

(and) 7. The moms will come to watch. The dads will come to watch.
The moms and the dads will come to watch.

Page 85

A Day at the Beach

> A **compound predicate** is two verbs joined by a conjunction and having the same subject.
> I went to the beach *and* swam in the ocean.

Underline the compound predicate in each of the following sentences and circle the conjunction.

1. On our trip to the beach, we went snorkeling (and) tried surfing.
2. We saw many beautiful fish (and) enjoyed the warm ocean water.
3. All day, the sun shone brightly (and) warmed us.
4. Mom and I lay on the beach (and) got a tan.
5. Dad and my little brother looked for shells (and) built a sand castle.
6. For dinner, we sat outside (and) ate hamburgers by the ocean.
7. Some people watched the waves (and) waited for the sunset.
8. Finally, the sun turned red (and) seemed to sink into the ocean.

Write four sentences about the beach that contain compound predicates.

1. Answers will vary.

2. _____

3. _____

4. _____

Page 86

The Tall Tulip Tale

> A **simple sentence** contains one independent clause. A **compound sentence** contains two independent clauses that are closely related, but which usually have different subjects. A conjunction usually, but not always, joins the two clauses in a compound sentence. Remember to put a comma after the first clause and before the conjunction that joins the two clauses. If the subject of the two clauses is the same, but is restated (usually with a pronoun) the sentence is still joined by a comma and conjunction.
> *simple:* Uncle Sid loves to garden.
> *compound:* Uncle Sid loves to garden, and Auntie Sue loves to fill their house with flowers.

On the line before each sentence, write S if it is a simple sentence; write C if it is a compound sentence. Place a comma in the correct part of each compound sentence.

S 1. Uncle Sid always plants tulip bulbs around the house.

C 2. Auntie Sue loves the tulips, and she looks forward to their blooming.

S 3. Uncle Sid put the bulbs in the ground in October.

S 4. All winter long, the sleeping tulips waited for the warm spring sun.

C 5. At last, they all began to push slowly through the earth, but one tulip burst through in a big way.

S 6. Underneath the kitchen window, an enormous yellow tulip grew rapidly.

S 7. Soon the plant grew past the window and hovered above the house.

C 8. Auntie Sue gasped, but fortunately she did not faint.

S 9. "Sid, come quick!" she shouted.

S 10. Uncle Sid stared up at the tulip and scratched his head.

C 11. Reporters arrived at the house, and Uncle Sid's amazing yellow tulip was on the evening news.

C 12. Uncle Sid told everyone that the huge flower had been a gift for his Sue, but that he didn't expect it to be quite so special.

S 13. Thanking him for her beautiful, tree-sized tulip, Auntie Sue gave Uncle Sid a big kiss.

Page 87

IF87132 *Grammar*

Deutschland

When two simple sentences with different subjects are combined by a conjunction, they form a **compound sentence**. A comma is usually always placed before the conjunction.

Uncle Otto danced in his lederhosen.   I joined in, too.
Uncle Otto danced in his lederhosen, and I joined in, too.

Tell whether each sentence is simple or compound by writing S (simple) or C (compound) on the line.

C 1. My parents speak German, and I love to listen to them.
S 2. Grandpa tells folk tales and sings German songs.
C 3. Sauerbraten is delicious, and I like to eat it often.
S 4. Many great composers and musicians have come from Germany.
C 5. Education in Germany is controlled by the states, but every child must go to school for at least nine or ten years.

Use a comma and the conjunction in parentheses to combine each pair of sentences. Write the compound sentence on the line.

1. My grandma makes homemade sauerkraut. I prefer red cabbage. (but)
   My grandma makes homemade sauerkraut, but I prefer red cabbage.
2. Do you plan to visit Germany? Would France appeal to you more? (or)
   Do you plan to visit Germany, or would France appeal to you more?
3. Berlin is Germany's capital. About three and a half million people live there. (and)
   Berlin is Germany's capital, and about three and a half million people live there.
4. My family is from New York. Our ancestors lived in the Thuringer Forest. (but)
   My family is from New York, but our ancestors lived in the Thuringer Forest.
5. The Black Forest is a mountainous region. The North German Plain is low and nearly flat. (but)
   The Black Forest is a mountainous region, but the North German Plain is low and nearly flat.

Page 88

Club Members Only

A **sentence** is a group of words containing a subject and a predicate and expressing a complete thought. A **fragment** is a group of words that does not express a complete thought. Fragments are missing either a subject or a verb.

My friends and I formed a special club. (sentence)
Helping other people. (fragment)

Write S before each group of words that is a sentence. Write F before each group of words that is a fragment.

S 1. Club members must use the secret password.
S 2. They greet other members with the secret handshake.
F 3. Every Saturday morning at the club treehouse.
S 4. Everyone shows kindness to all club members.
S 5. Club members bring fifty cents to every Saturday meeting for the Helping Fund.
F 6. When the Helping Fund gets really full.
S 7. We will spend the Fund money to help someone out.
S 8. Members vote on the best way to spend the money we have collected.
S 9. Sometimes we will do volunteer projects.
F 10. Raking leaves or pulling weeds for elderly people.
F 11. Other jobs too.
S 12. Our motto is "To help others above all."
S 13. Occasionally, we just hang out and have fun.
F 14. Skating in the school parking lot or eating at the clubhouse once in a while.
S 15. It is fun.
F 16. Being a club member.

Page 89

Mother Nature

A **run-on** is two or more complete sentences written without proper punctuation. Run-on sentences may be corrected by breaking the sentence, by utilizing a semi-colon, or by adding a comma and a conjunction. The semicolon and the comma-conjunction pair should only be used when the ideas in the run-on are closely related. A comma should never be used without a conjunction to correct a run-on.

run-on: Reneé is skillfull, he likes to garden.
***correct:** Reneé is skillful. He likes to garden.*
run-on: Joey is usually serious he is funny sometimes.
***correct:** Joey is usually serious, but he is funny sometimes.*

Read the following sentences and determine if they are run-ons or not. If the sentence is a run-on, write **RO** in the blank before the sentence. If not, write **C** for correct.

RO 1. Raking leaves is not easy, you must work for a long time in the cold outdoors.
C 2. I love to go fishing; it invigorates me.
RO 3. He had just seen a skunk, it was coming down the street.
C 4. Maria plants flowers and raises vegetables in her garden.
RO 5. Ramón loves books about birds he just read one about bald eagles.
RO 6. Kyle likes to mountain climb, he is afraid of heights.
C 7. Patricia collects leaves, and she presses them in a book.
RO 8. I want to go hiking, I also want to go bird watching.

Correct the run-on sentences on the lines below.

1. Janice stole my ant farm, she set all the ants free.
   Janice stole my ant farm, and she set all the ants free.
2. My mom loves petunias she likes to plant them in window boxes.
   My mom loves petunias. She likes to plant them in window boxes.
3. Our first garden was very large, planting all those vegetables was hard work.
   Our first garden was very large. Planting all those vegetables was hard work.
4. Soon we will harvest our tomatoes, I just love fresh tomato sauce!
   Soon we will harvest our tomatoes. I just love fresh tomato sauce!

Page 90

It's in the Bag

There are four types of sentences.

Declarative —A declarative sentence makes a statement and ends with a period.
Interrogative —An interrogative sentence asks a question and ends with a question mark.
Imperative —An imperative sentence commands or requests. It ends with a period or an exclamation point. The subject *you* is always implied.
Exclamatory —An exclamatory sentence can either be a statement or a command made with strong feeling. It ends with an exclamation point.

declarative: There is a paper bag on the table.
interrogative: What is in that bag?
imperative: Take the bag off the table.
exclamatory: Be careful not to drop it!

Write the number of each sentence inside the correct bag to identify the sentence type.

1. What's in the bag?
2. It sounds like it is moving.
3. Look and see.
4. Whoa, be careful!
5. Do you think it's alive?
6. I don't dare look.
7. Just hurry up and open the bag!
8. Please hand me that stick.
9. Whenever I poke the bag, it makes a scratching noise.
10. Shhh!
11. Are you ever going to look inside that thing?
12. Wow, it's a rat!
13. It must be food for Ronald's snake.
14. I think that's gross!
15. Should I set him free?
16. Let me do it.

Declarative: 2 6 13 9
Interrogative: 1 5 11 15
Imperative: 3 7 8 16
Exclamatory: 4 10 12 14

Page 91

It's a Bug's Life

A **declarative sentence** makes a statement and ends with a period.
Catching bugs is fun.

For each of the following sentences, add the proper punctuation. Write **yes** if it is a declarative sentence; write **no** if it is not.

no 1. Is that a stink bug
yes 2. Some insects called bugs are not really bugs
yes 3. Not all insects are bugs
no 4. Are bedbugs really bugs
yes 5. Many birds eat bugs
no 6. Take that ugly bug outside please
yes 7. Junebugs are not bugs
yes 8. My sister really bugs me
no 9. Do you think ants are bugs
yes 10. My stepsister Lucy gets totally freaked out by most bugs
no 11. What is the difference between an insect and a bug
yes 12. Bugs are very useful little creatures, even if they are slightly pesky
yes 13. Some bugs suck blood from animals and plants
no 14. Are you feeling itchy
no 15. Don't let the bedbugs bite
yes 16. All bugs are insects
no 17. How many legs do bugs have
yes 18. Bugs have two pair of different wings

Page 92

Who Are You?

An **interrogative sentence** asks a question and ends with a question mark.
What is an interrogative sentence?

For each of the following sentences, write **yes** if it is interrogative or **no** if it is not. Add ending punctuation. Then, answer each question with a *declarative* sentence of your own.

no 1. State your full name.
yes 2. When were you born?
yes 3. In which city and state were you born?
yes 4. Who are the other people in your family?
no 5. State the name of your first teacher.
yes 6. What is your favorite subject at school?
no 7. List your hobbies.
yes 8. With whom do you like to spend your time?
no 9. Describe your greatest talent.
yes 10. What is the very best thing about you?
yes 11. Whom would you most like to to be like?
no 12. Explain what job you hope to have when you are an adult.

Declarative Sentences will vary.

Page 93

Sudsing Up

An **imperative sentence** commands or requests. It ends with a period or an exclamation point. The subject *you* is always implied.
Wash the car.

In the following sentences, write **yes** if it is imperative; write **no** if it is not.

When You Wash A Car Remember:
yes 1. Don't forget to roll up the window.
yes 2. Use a soft sponge.
yes 3. Please avoid harsh detergents.
no 4. Your car will look best if you wash the windows too.
no 5. Water spots do not look good.
yes 6. Always dry the car off completely.

Change each one of the following questions into commands or requests. Be sure to use correct capitalization and the proper punctuation.

1. Could you please help me wash the car?
Please help me wash the car.

2. Will you bring the bucket here?
Bring the bucket here.

3. Do you mind filling it with soap and water?
Fill it with soap and water.

4. Will you wash the tires with that brush please?
Please wash the tires with that brush.

5. Will you wait until I finish sudsing up the car?
Wait until I finish sudsing up the car.

6. Would you please rinse the soap off with the sprayer?
Please rinse the soap off with the sprayer.

7. Do you mind helping me dry off the car?
Help me dry off the car.

8. Will you accept $10.00 for helping me?
Accept $10.00 for helping me.

Page 94

A Close Call

An **exclamatory sentence** can be either a statement or a command made with strong feeling. It ends with an exclamation point.
Wait just one minute!
You've got to be kidding!
Look out!

Add ending punctuation to the following sentences. Then put a star next to each exclamatory sentence.

Answers may vary slightly.

1. My dog, tony, is a poodle.
2. He doesn't like to be touched.
3. Oh no, he's mad now! ★
4. Please don't pester the dog.
5. Stop it right now! ★
6. What if he bites you?
7. Sit tony.
8. Leave him alone.
9. Ow! ★
10. It's okay tony; settle down.
11. Pass the dog treats please.
12. Whoa, that was a close call! ★
13. At least he didn't break the skin.

Page 95

Rain, Rain, Don't Go Away!

A **comma** is used...
- to set off an introductory phrase or independent clause.
  - *After a hard rain, the earth smells fresh.*
- after introductory words or phrases such as *yes, indeed, well, in addition, thus,* and *moreover.*
  - *Yes, it is supposed to rain today.*
- after words of direct address.
  - *Melissa, come play in the rain with me.*
- in a series—to separate words.
  - *I have a raincoat, boots, and an umbrella.*

Add commas to the following sentences.

Yes, I love a rainy day!

The rain taps on the windows, plays on the sidewalk, and dances on the roof.

I watch, wait, and wonder what the warm rain will bring.

Maxi, why don't you hop up here and enjoy the rain with me.

My cat hopped onto the windowsill, began purring, and fell asleep.

No, she didn't care about the falling raindrops at all.

For the next hour or so, I snuggled into the window seat and listened to the rain's song.

Its song is sweet, steady, and strong.

"Sara, come down for dinner," Mom called.

As I left my room, I whispered to the rain,

"Rain, please don't go away!"

Page 96

Maxwell T. Stewart

Use two commas to set off interrupting words or expressions and appositive phrases.
You can see, I'm sure, that rats spread disease.
The rat, a nocturnal animal, sleeps all day.

Add commas to the following sentences.

1. Maxwell, the lazy rat, slept all day in the alley behind Tony's Pizzeria.

2. He hid during the day, under the steps by the back door.

3. No one, including the other rats, ever bothered him.

4. He, Maxwell T. Stewart, called himself King of the Rats.

5. This rat king, a real scoundrel, was bigger and fiercer than any other alley rat.

6. At night, when the darkness came, Maxwell prowled.

7. The nightlife, especially the smells of the pizzeria, brought him out.

8. He rummaged through the best eateries in town, the local trash cans.

9. After a night of indulging, Maxwell grew fat and sleepy.

10. Maxwell T. Stewart, King of the Rats, slinked past the other alley creatures and into his home beneath the steps of Tony's Pizzeria.

Page 97

Mom's Photo Album

When writing a **date**, use a **comma** to separate the day of the week from the month. A comma also separates the date from the year.
Wednesday, February 3, 1999
Tuesday, April 13, 1993

Capitalize and add commas to the dates below.

Wednesday, February 14, 1968

Tuesday, September 4, 1973

Monday, May 30, 1977

Thursday, December 25, 1980

Wednesday, August 28, 1985

Sunday, November 27, 1988

Wednesday, March 20, 1991

Saturday, July 4, 1992

Thursday, October 31, 1996

Sunday, April 4, 1999

Saturday, January 1, 2000

Tuesday, February 13, 2001

Page 98

Mailbag

When writing an address, use a comma to separate the name of the city from the name of the state or country. Never put a comma between the state and the zip code.
Miss Spinella Spider
8542 Thread Lane
Web Corner, California 90210

Write the addresses correctly on the envelopes to the right. Don't forget capitals and punctuation.

From: mr and mrs thomas cat
1234 feline drive
meowville texas 56543

To: marvin mouse sr
873 rodent road
squeaker town new york 38214

Mr. and Mrs. Thomas Cat
1234 Feline Drive
Meowville, Texas 56543

Marvin Mouse, Sr.
873 Rodent Road
Squeaker Town, New York 38214

From: dr harold hedgehog
7117 bristle boulevard
prickly park wisconsin 87675

To: miss priscilla porcupine
111 aquilla avenue
smart city minnesota 75320

Dr. Harold Hedgehog
7117 Bristle Boulevard
Prickly Park, Wisconsin 87675

Miss Priscilla Porcupine
111 Aquilla Avenue
Smart City, Minnesota 75320

From: freddy falcon
2020 laguna landings
cliffside california 27022

To: wise old owl
42 hoot lane
treehole maine 40000

Freddy Falcon
2020 Laguna Landings
Cliffside, California 27022

Wise Old Owl
42 Hoot Lane
Treehole, Maine 40000

Page 99

We Wanna Know Your Name

Use a capital letter and a period for a title that is abbreviated. Use a capital and a period when an initial is used in place of a person's name. Always put a comma before a title if it appears after a person's name.

Roger T. Applegate, Jr.
Dr. Katherine R. Williams

Rewrite the following names and initials correctly inside the name tags.

mrs o sanford
HELLO MY NAME IS: Mrs. O. Sanford

dr philip prince
Dr. Philip Prince

bj taylor jr
B.J. Taylor, Jr.

capt douglas walker
Capt. Douglas Walker

marco garcia sr
Marco Garcia, Sr.

gov george r rice
VOTE FOR Gov. George R. Rice

miss mz vandermeer
Miss M.Z. Vandermeer

rev james tiesdale
Rev. James Tiesdale

carlos j lucas jr
Carlos J. Lucas, Jr.

prof rr chapman
Prof. R.R. Chapman

maj michael b paris
Maj. Michael B. Paris

adm juliet n love
Adm. Juliet N. Love

Page 100

Borice's Book Bag

Capitalize and underline or italicize the titles of books, magazines, and newspapers. The first word, the last word, and all other important words in a title are capitalized. Articles (the), conjunctions (and) and prepositions (of) are not capitalized unless they are the first or last word of the title.

Out of the Dust
People
The Chicago Tribune

Rewrite the titles from Borice's book bag correctly on the corresponding lines below.

1. hatchet
2. a light in the attic
3. where the red fern grows
4. the moves make the man
5. east elementary's news
6. maniac magee
7. the adventures of tom sawyer
8. the changing desert
9. doll collectors' magazine
10. dinosaurs of north america
11. sports illustrated
12. teen magazine
13. the lincoln herald
14. the detroit free press
15. national geographic

1. *Hatchet*
2. *A Light in the Attic*
3. *Where the Red Fern Grows*
4. *The Moves Make the Man*
5. *East Elementary's News*
6. *Maniac Magee*
7. *The Adventures of Tom Sawyer*
8. *The Changing Desert*
9. *Doll Collector's Magazine*
10. *Dinosaur's of North America*
11. *Sports Illustrated*
12. *Teen Magazine*
13. *The Lincoln Herald*
14. *The Detroit Free Press*
15. *National Geographic*

Page 101

The Long and Short of It

Abbreviations of proper nouns are capitalized. Abbreviations of common nouns are not. Special titles and degrees are also capitalized. Abbreviations should not be used in sentences.

Senator = Sen.   centimeter = cm

Write the abbreviations for the following words.

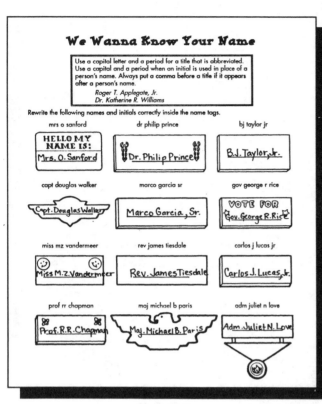

feet — ft.
Senior — Sr.
Monday — Mon.
street — St.
Tuesday — Tues.
ounce — oz.
August — Aug.

November — Nov.
Junior — Jr.
Misses — Mrs.
avenue — ave.
Reverend — Rev.
inch — in.
Wednesday — Wed.

Captain — Capt.
September — Sept.
court — ct.
January — Jan.
week — wk.
Saturday — Sat.
year — yr.

dozen — dz.
Mister — Mr.
December — Dec.
pound — lb.
Friday — Fri.
month — mo.
Sunday — Sun.

et cetera — etc.
February — Feb.
Thursday — Thurs.
yard — yd.
October — Oct.
mile — m.
Doctor — Dr.

Page 102

Chocolate Caramel Divine

Quotation marks are used to enclose direct quotation. The end punctuation of the sentence usually comes before the final quotation mark at the end of the quote.
Always capitalize the first word of direct quotation. Do not capitalize the first word in an interrupted quote, unless the second part begins a new sentence.

"It is time to go to the store!" Mom announced.
"When we get there," she continued, "pick out your favorite ice cream."
"We won't forget." replied Nate. "We love ice cream."

Add the correct punctuation and capitalization to the following sentences. Write the corrected sentences on the lines.

1. would you help me choose some ice cream asked chloe
"Would you help me choose some ice cream?" asked Chloe.
2. sure answered nate let's get something with caramel
"Sure," answered Nate. "Let's get something with caramel."
3. caramel is good replied chloe but i prefer chocolate
"Caramel is good," replied Chloe, "but I prefer chocolate."
4. how about something with both suggested nate
"How about something with both," suggested Nate.
5. that's a great idea chloe responded
"That's a great idea," Chloe responded.
6. hey said nate i found one called chocolate caramel divine
"Hey," said Nate, "I found one called Chocolate Caramel Divine."
7. that sounds perfect chloe agreed
"That sounds perfect," Chloe agreed.
8. where are you going now nate shouted
"Where are you going now?" Nate shouted.
9. to get some hot fudge to pour on top chloe yelled back
"To get some hot fudge to pour on top!" Chloe yelled back.
10. don't forget a jar of caramel too nate called
"Don't forget a jar of caramel, too!" Nate called.

Page 103

IF87132 *Grammar*